D1398931

POST-TRAUMATIC STRESS DISORDER (PTSD)

DEALING WITH TRAGEDY

Carolyn Simpson and Dwain Simpson

The Rosen Publishing Group, Inc.
New York

In memory of Pamela Jessica Runyon

Published in 1997, 2002 by The Rosen Publishing Group, Inc.
29 East 21st Street, New York, NY 10010

Revised Edition 2002

Library of Congress Cataloging-in-Publication Data

Simpson, Carolyn.
Coping with post-traumatic stress disorder: dealing with tragedy / Carolyn Simpson and Dwain Simpson. — Rev. ed.
p. cm. — (Coping)
Includes bibliographical references and index.
Summary: Discusses such situations as physical abuse, natural disasters, wars, and violence, that can cause stressful responses and describes ways of dealing with these delayed reactions to trauma.
ISBN 0-8239-3456-X
1. Post-traumatic stress disorder—Juvenile literature.
[1. Post-traumatic stress disorder.]
I. Simpson, Dwain, 1951– II. Title. III. Series.
RC552.P67 S456 2002
616.85'21—dc21

2001006831

Manufactured in the United States of America

Contents

Introduction: What Is PTSD?

Lower Manhattan, September 11, 2001, 8:45 AM*. Tim was drinking his second cup of coffee of the morning and preparing for a nine o'clock meeting with his boss. As he was gathering the necessary files, he noticed the sound of a jet airplane's engines. The sound was not unusual, exactly, but something was not quite right. He suddenly realized that it sounded far too close. In the very next moment he heard an enormous crash and was knocked off his feet onto the floor, which was shuddering beneath him. As soon as the building stopped shaking, Tim rose carefully and hesitantly approached his office window. He could not believe what he saw: The north tower of the World Trade Center had an enormous gash across it, from which black, billowing smoke and flames were pouring into the clear blue sky. The plane he heard must have accidentally crashed into the tower! Soon his officemates and boss congregated in the conference room and made sure everyone was all right and accounted for. A feeling of nervous relief spread through the room as everyone began recounting what they had seen and heard.*

This brief moment of calm was shattered a few minutes later, however, when they heard the sound of another jet approaching. From the conference room window, they all witnessed the unimaginable: a second plane smashing into the south tower of the World Trade Center. The horror of this sight was compounded by the sickening realization that this was no accident; New York City was being attacked!

Not knowing if more planes were on the way, Tim's boss immediately ordered everyone to evacuate the building, which stood just across the street from the World Trade Center. As the entire company hurried into the stairwell, they were joined by hundreds of the building's other occupants. While there was some jostling, yelling, and crying, most people proceeded in an orderly fashion and helped those who were experiencing difficulty in descending. The twelve-flight journey seemed to take an hour, though it could not have lasted for more than ten minutes.

The real horror was still ahead of Tim, however. After reaching the lobby of his building and exiting onto the street, he was startled by the sound of piercing shrieks from nearby pedestrians. As if in a nightmare, he noticed bodies lying motionless on the street. When he looked up at the burning towers, he understood why some people were screaming and why others were lying on the ground. Bodies were falling through the sky. People were jumping from the top floors of the towers!

At this point, Tim blacked out. He must have kept walking but has no recollection of his movements and no idea how much time passed. The next thing he remembered was finding himself walking uptown ten blocks north of his office building. His clothes were covered in ash. He was hearing police officers and firefighters urging everyone to run as fast as they could. Apparently one of the towers was falling down. He received this information calmly, numbed by all that he had seen. All he could do was keep walking; he couldn't run. None of it seemed to matter anymore.

For a week after the attack on the towers, Tim talked to almost no one and did not leave his home except to walk his dog. He cried for extended periods, felt alternately depressed and extremely anxious, and had nightmares about being trapped in a collapsing building. Several weeks later, the sound of an airplane overhead still brought on a sense of panic. He could not bring himself to enter tall buildings, and he refused to use elevators. Anytime he smelled smoke or heard a siren, he felt like he had been thrown right back into the chaotic, terrifying nightmare of that September morning.

Celinda's mother would not let her work in fast-food restaurants or all-night convenience stores because she worried that these places might get robbed. Even though Celinda was seventeen and thought she should decide for herself where she worked that summer, she humored her mother and took a filing job at a credit union. It never occurred to either of them that she would be in danger there.

Celinda usually took her lunch break at 1:00 PM, but on this particular day she left early to meet some friends. Back at work earlier than usual, she was sitting at a desk in the corner of the lobby around 1:20 PM when a man walked into the credit union. She'd just been thinking there wasn't a single customer in the lobby; no wonder they preferred her to take her lunch break at this hour. She frowned as she watched the man turn around and lock the front door. That was an odd thing to do, she thought. When he turned back around, he had pulled a stocking cap over his face.

Before she could figure out what was happening, a second man materialized as if out of nowhere and was rounding up the people in the back offices. The first man pointed a gun at the two tellers and ordered them to start stuffing money into the burlap bags he tossed them. "Don't even think about it," he growled as one of the tellers slid her hand under the counter and fumbled for the panic button.

He looked over at Celinda. "You," he said, "get over here with them."

Celinda was herded with the other office workers into the vault. At the last minute, he yanked Celinda aside. He locked the vault and dragged Celinda to where the tellers were. His accomplice had bagged the money and was tying up the two women. "Don't hurt us, please," one was begging. He gagged her. The first guy was busy tying Celinda's hands behind her back. He shoved her down onto the floor hard and then tied her ankles together. Before the men turned to leave, they shot the tellers at point-blank range.

Celinda braced for the next inevitable gunshot. It never came. She heard the back door open and shut, and then it was quiet. She lay still, watching the blood pool around the tellers. She was afraid if she moved, they would come back and shoot her, too. She waited for what seemed like an hour, hardly breathing, hardly moving. Maybe they weren't coming back.

She wiggled her wrists against the rope. If she could get her hands free, she could call for help. She twisted her arms, but the rope was very tight.

The women who had been shot looked dead. Their lips were blue, and the blood had stopped flowing. Celinda did not want to look at them. Somehow she managed to stand up by first struggling to her knees and then pushing up with her feet. She edged over to the counter and found the panic button. She turned around and lifted her bound hands up high enough behind her to reach the button. Then she pushed it.

When the police arrived, they hailed Celinda as a hero. She did not feel like one, though; she felt sick to her stomach. She was chilled to the bone, even when she stepped out into the sunshine. It did not matter that they caught the men robbing another bank two weeks later; she was too afraid to return to the credit union that summer. She would not even set foot in a bank to cash her last paycheck. She took sleeping pills to make her sleep at night, which was the worst time of the day for her. Every time she shut her eyes, she saw the tellers lying curled up on the floor, the blood running out of both the gunshot wounds and their mouths.

Most of the time, people hear about post-traumatic stress disorder (PTSD) and assume that the victim is a combat veteran. While wartime vets initially brought this disorder to our attention, they are far from the only ones to experience symptoms. Anyone who has been involved in a car accident, robbery, terrorist act, or earthquake may suffer from PTSD, too. Those who have been abused over a long period of time suffer even more intensely. In 1980, the American Psychiatric Association included for the first time the category of post-traumatic stress disorder in its official diagnostic manual of mental disorders. PTSD is a stressed reaction to a traumatic event, such as being held hostage, being sexually or physically abused, or seeing loved ones burned in a fire or battered by a rampaging tornado.

What Is Post-Traumatic Stress Disorder?

Post-traumatic stress disorder, or PTSD, can result from a person experiencing an unusual and frightening event that simply overwhelms his or her ability to cope with it. Sometimes the person is actually hurt, or sometimes, as with Celinda, the person just thinks he or she is going to be hurt or killed. Other times, as in Tim's case, a person sees other people dying, and the experience and memories are so horrific that he or she can't cope with them.

We will show you in the first section of this book some of the many events that can overwhelm a person's ability to cope. You can probably think of a few instances yourself: the attacks on the World Trade Center and the Pentagon on September 11, 2001; the recent school shootings in Santee, California, or Littleton, Colorado; the Oklahoma

City bombing of 1995; and the tornadoes that regularly tear through the Midwest and South. The events that cause the most problems for people are the ones that are done on purpose by other humans. Violent acts of nature, of course, are terrifying, but people hurting other people intentionally and repeatedly create the most horror. Chronic abuse, whether physical, sexual, or emotional, is the single most traumatic experience of all, especially if the abuser is someone the victim is dependent upon.

Childhood abuse very often leads to symptoms of PTSD; it also disrupts the child's opportunity to master appropriate developmental tasks, such as learning to trust people and developing a sense of initiative and competence. If a person is abused during childhood, he may never develop the ability to soothe himself; he may not see the world as a safe place and may not know how to trust people, which only sets him up for further exploitation.

Estimates suggest about 5 percent of Americans—that is more than 13 million people—have PTSD at any given moment in time. Of the general population, experts estimate that between 14 and 43 percent of boys and girls have experienced at least one traumatic event sufficient to cause PTSD.

The basic symptoms of PTSD are similar to responses to any kind of traumatic event. Children and adults suffer alike, although kids are not as prone to suffering flashbacks. All, in varying degrees, suffer from the three cardinal signs of PTSD: hyperarousal (always being on guard against danger), intrusion (thinking about the traumatic experience over and over, or trying not to think about it at all), and constriction (numbing your thoughts and avoiding others so you do not relive the traumatic event).

Aside from hyperarousal, intrusion, and constriction, people who suffer from PTSD also experience physical signs, such as headaches, stomach problems, dizziness, chest pain, and racing heartbeat, as well as fatigue and difficulty sleeping; emotional signs, such as feelings of helplessness, hopelessness, numbness, indecisiveness, shortened attention span, and poor impulse control; and interpersonal signs, such as irritability, isolation from others, and the tendency to be distant and/or controlling with others.

PTSD is diagnosed when a person's symptoms last longer than a month. Sometimes symptoms do not show up until months after the actual event. After the September 11 attacks on the World Trade Center and the Pentagon, George Bonanno, a clinical psychologist at Columbia University who specializes in grief and trauma, told the *New York Times,* "Just because someone isn't feeling stressed right now doesn't necessarily mean they won't have trauma symptoms two months from now." The article points out that trauma experts have no way of knowing who will suffer from PTSD and who will somehow find a way to cope and move on following a given tragedy. Generally, 25 percent of people who have experienced a traumatic event will still be exhibiting symptoms of traumatic stress three months later. That percentage may increase if there is a sense that the event might be repeated, as in the case of terrorist attacks, natural disasters, or abuse. As Dr. Russell J. Kormann, a post-traumatic stress specialist at Rutgers University's Anxiety Disorders Clinic, said in the *New York Times* of the World Trade Center attacks, "This is uncharted territory. We don't have an idea who is going to be affected and to what degree. It's something thousands of people will be dealing with for years to come."

This book looks at the different events, such as war, terrorism, disasters, abuse, captivity, and violence, that can lead to PTSD. Some experiences lead to more alarming symptoms, such as trancelike behavior, and others provoke symptoms that do not occur until many years later. But what is important to remember is that PTSD is a treatable condition. You can get better once you are ready to deal with the memories of the traumatic event. That is the good news; the bad news is that you will never heal if you simply pretend that the trauma never took place or that it was not bad enough to warrant such anxiety on your part. Our memories play tricks on us, distorting time and sequence, but rarely do they materialize out of nowhere. And while they may go underground for weeks, months, or even years, the memories never completely go away.

Complete recovery from PTSD occurs within three months in approximately half of all cases that are treated. Many other sufferers have symptoms that may last longer than twelve months. It is necessary to confront your traumatic memories to get on with your life. If you know what to expect when confronting your memories, you will be better able to tolerate the anxiety that goes along with them. It is to that end—educating you about PTSD—that we've written this book.

Part I:
What Causes PTSD?

Violent Acts of Nature

On May 3, 1999, Phillip was sitting in his living room watching with grim interest the news about a giant tornado heading for Oklahoma City, Oklahoma. Although people in the Midwest have a healthy respect for tornadoes, no one expected a tornado that size to hit a major city. Surely it would quickly die out as it struck buildings and houses.

Phillip's wife, Ann, did some chores around the house while Phillip continued to watch the news.

The sky grew dark; the weather forecasters predicted the tornado would indeed strike Oklahoma City, and Phillip's house lay right in its current path. Still, he could not imagine that he was in danger.

Suddenly the lights flickered and went out; the television died. Phillip ran to his front door and pulled it open. There in the distance, but advancing toward him quickly, was the biggest, blackest cloud he had ever seen. It stretched across the whole space in front of him. He knew he could not run anywhere now; it was coming straight at them.

Phillip and Ann took shelter in a closet on the ground floor of their two-story home. They huddled together as the massive tornado engulfed their house. They could hear the roar of the wind as it blew out all their windows. They watched in horror as the dirt blew in under the closet door; they crouched as low as possible and clung to each other as the wind tried to suck them out of the closet. Phillip remembers most clearly the smell of wet dirt permeating the air. He could even taste it. It seemed like the wind raged around them for hours, as furniture banged against the walls. Then, suddenly, it was quiet. The tornado was gone.

Phillip and Ann tentatively opened the closet door. When they stepped into the hallway, they realized they were looking up at the sky. The whole second floor of their house had been swept away. All the windows were blown out on the first floor; their belongings—books, lamps, dishes—were strewn about and broken.

Phillip opened the front door to check on the rest of the neighborhood. He had been one of the lucky ones. The other houses had been flattened to their foundations. The news confirmed later that they had ridden out an F-5 tornado, the largest kind.

That is not the end of the story. Imagine how Phillip felt whenever he heard the wind pick up; imagine his anxiety when he smelled wet dirt or dreamed he was tasting it again. For weeks and weeks, Phillip and Ann had trouble sleeping at night. They sold what was left of their property and moved away.

Survivor Guilt

Marjorie survived a fire when she was seven years old, but her baby sister did not. Marjorie carried her guilt—both for surviving and for not saving her sister—for the rest of her life.

No one knows how the fire started; some think the electrical wiring was faulty. Whatever the case, Marjorie awoke one night, coughing and gasping as smoke billowed around her. She called to her parents, but no one replied. In the terror of the moment, she had forgotten that her mother was working a night shift and her father was away on business. Her two other sisters in the room began to cry and cough, too.

Marjorie was not the oldest, but she was the most alert. She knew what to do. Crawling on the floor toward the door, she beckoned to her sisters to follow her. She led them down the hallway to the front door. The fire was raging upstairs where her parents' bedroom and baby sister's crib were. She was torn; should she go up those stairs and pull the baby out of the crib? Her throat hurt from the smoke, and her sisters were panicking. Marjorie led them out of the house. She could hear the wail of the fire trucks in the distance. Someone had called the fire department. Help would come. Neighbors ran across the lawn to scoop up the girls. Marjorie turned back. "I've got to get the baby," she cried.

The neighbors tried to grab her. "You can't go back in there," they said. Nevertheless, Marjorie pulled away from them and ran to the front door. She pulled it open and shuddered as the heat hit her. By now the stairs were engulfed in flames. No one could run up those stairs to get the baby unless he or she could walk through fire.

Marjorie backed up. Someone had brought her mother home from work. Her mother was screaming in a high-pitched wail, "Where's my baby?" She was crying, and Marjorie felt personally responsible for leaving the baby behind.

By now the fire trucks had arrived, and the firefighters threw ladders against the house, climbing in vain to save the baby girl they knew was still inside on the second floor. Marjorie sat in a daze watching. Her mother wrapped her arms around Julie, Marjorie's older sister, and hugged her to her chest. She kept on wailing—such an awful sound to Marjorie—"Save my baby!" "Save her, please!" "Don't let her die!"

Marjorie's mother kept screaming even when a fireman carried the lifeless baby out and tried to perform CPR on her. Marjorie heard it all, and she felt responsible. She had let her little baby sister, who was not able to crawl out of her crib, die. Their house burned to the ground. They lost everything.

Marjorie never blamed her mother for being at work and leaving the girls to fend for themselves. She didn't blame her father for being out of town, and she didn't even blame her older sister for not trying to save their youngest sister. No, Marjorie blamed herself because she had looked up those stairs before the flames engulfed them and had decided not to run up them to try to find her. Marjorie felt she was the only one who'd had a chance of saving her youngest sister.

Many years later, Marjorie was grown up, and she was my client. She was both depressed (anguished, actually) and anxious. She could not relax; she would start to fall asleep and then bolt up in bed, thinking she smelled smoke. Once she had started a small fire on the stove and practically came unglued, screaming at the top of her lungs, and drenching the food under a thick layer of fire retardant. She had never talked to anyone else about the fire that night so long ago; it had become a family secret. It was just too overwhelming to discuss. So the trauma festered inside her, preventing her from moving on with her life.

How PTSD Affects a Person

Horrible experiences can create permanent mental pictures. They are frightening and traumatic, and our minds play them for us over and over again. If we try to push them aside, they come back to haunt us in dreams and nightmares. Shock and utter helplessness combine to make the brain automatically imprint these memories—and not just the memories, but all the feelings that accompanied the trauma at the time. Because of the mind's capacity to remember and relive the experience, people with post-traumatic stress disorder usually suffer from three major symptoms: hyperarousal, intrusion, and constriction.

Hyperarousal is always being on guard against danger. People who have suffered a traumatic experience will startle easily, react irritably to things that would not ordinarily bother them, and sleep poorly. Some cannot fall asleep, while others fall asleep but cannot sleep for very long. They are startled awake by every little noise in the house. It is as if these people are always on the alert for danger.

Intrusion is when a person keeps reliving the trauma. Bad memories are not always that easy to dismiss. People have flashbacks; they see the whole event happening in their minds and believe they are experiencing it again. Many combat veterans hear noises or see things that trigger their memories, and they start reexperiencing the whole traumatic event. Younger people do not seem to have flashbacks as often because they tend to daydream about, and thus consciously reexperience, the trauma they have suffered. Older adolescents and adults, who perhaps are trying to forget the memories, are more prone to having flashbacks.

Flashbacks can also manifest themselves as feelings that are inappropriate to the present occasion. If you feel overwhelmingly sad when nothing sad is occurring, but you had suffered a trauma in the past, clearly the memories of the feelings you experienced are intruding into your awareness. Flashbacks can take the form of physical sensations, feelings, and smells. When my client who survived the fire constantly smelled smoke when there was none around, that was a flashback.

Some people are having a flashback when they stop feeling anything at all. This is called constriction, or numbness, the third symptom of PTSD (it will be discussed shortly). For children who survived years of physical, sexual, or emotional trauma, that is typically the tool they used to cope during the actual abuse. They stopped feeling; they went numb until the abuse was over. Years later, adults who were abused as children may feel themselves going numb again; they are having a flashback.

Intrusion occurs when the memory of the trauma keeps reinserting itself into the victim's awareness. People suffering from PTSD do not just have nightmares; they have repetitive nightmares. The nightmares may not all be exactly alike, but the themes will be the same. Children usually play out their traumas over and over without understanding what they are doing. Several children who were kidnapped and buried alive back in the 1980s later played "kidnapper tag" with their friends. Others kept burying their Barbie dolls or taking them for rides on "kidnapped vans." This kind of repetitive play is called reenacting the trauma; it is obsessive and monotonous. Older people may reenact their traumas by getting into relationships that duplicate the abuse experienced in their pasts.

The third PTSD symptom is constriction, or numbing. Because traumatic memories are so intrusive, people resort to different tactics to be able to tolerate this assault. Some people just turn off their feelings. Someone cannot wipe away a memory that the brain has imprinted, but he or she can numb himself or herself to the feelings that were stored with the memory. The bad thing about turning off feelings is that someone cannot selectively turn off the scary or sad feelings and hang onto good feelings. If someone numbs himself or herself, he or she loses all feelings. Many with PTSD seem to be flat; they do not show excitement, happiness, or joy because they have numbed themselves to sadness, horror, and fear. In an attempt to create some safety in their lives and to manage their fears, many traumatized people restrict their lives. They avoid anything that might trigger their bad memories. They avoid relationships because it hurts to love and lose people.

People with PTSD suffer from a variety of feelings, including shame, guilt, and anger. Phillip and his wife switch between anger and grief: They lost most of their belongings; they tell themselves they should have heeded the weather forecasters and left earlier with their most precious possessions. Marjorie struggles with guilt every day of her life; she "should have saved her sister." Underneath her guilt is anger that her parents were not there and that she was thrown into such a position of responsibility for which she was too young.

People who have witnessed others dying during a disaster have to work through the stages of grief, in addition to their feelings about the trauma. Grieving time is not the same for everyone. At first, survivors experience shock and denial. They tell themselves the tragic event did not happen, or that it was not really so bad. Shock eventually gives way to anger, as if their outrage can undo the injustice of what happened. Anger covers the sadness and recognition of the loss. Once the loss is mourned, it can be accepted. The victim is then ready to get on with his or her life.

Consequences of PTSD for the Self

Sleep disorders are very common with victims of PTSD. They suffer either from insomnia (the inability to fall asleep or stay asleep) or nightmares. If they cannot get any rest at night, they will probably become jittery, irritable, and/or impulsive.

Some individuals become anxious or depressed. Those who spend their time worrying about the trauma and trying to avoid its recurrence belong to the first category. Those who give in to a feeling of helplessness are depressed.

Many times victims succumb to free-floating anger. Anger becomes a significant problem for many people who suffered trauma at an early age. The child may never develop the capacity to regulate his emotions; he may not be able to soothe himself, and so he may easily become overwhelmed by later stressful events and prone to excessive anger and rage. Chemical changes in the brain of the person suffering from PTSD may make him more on edge to begin with and primed to "go off" with little provocation.

Paranoia is another PTSD symptom. It makes a person seem unjustly suspicious. People who are paranoid may seem unusually jumpy because they are always on guard for another disaster. Victims of weather-related catastrophes may come to fear the weather conditions that precipitated the disaster. People traumatized by tornadoes often get panicky when dark clouds loom on the horizon or a sudden cold gust of wind stirs the leaves on trees. People who have survived fires are nervous around flames, even when the fire is safely confined to a fireplace.

Being anxious all of the time is nerve-racking and hard on your body. Victims of PTSD suffer overwhelmingly from ulcers, high blood pressure, and—if they have turned to drugs and alcohol to help alleviate their pain—the physical complications of substance abuse. Drugs, including alcohol, have a numbing effect on emotions. Unfortunately, they cause more problems, such as addiction, impaired driving (which can lead to incarceration), broken relationships, overdoses, and even death. People often turn to drugs to suppress the immediate feelings of panic in the aftermath of a trauma. Initially, these substances cause fear and anxiety to go away, and victims mistake these reactions for relief. Soon, they need to use more and more drugs to maintain the reprieve. They may become addicted, actually needing the alcohol or drug to keep from facing the pain of withdrawal.

Addiction has its own set of problems. Alcoholics face alcohol poisoning, liver disease, and stomach problems. People can drink themselves to death. Drug addicts require increasing amounts of the drug they are abusing in order to control their symptoms, but they can die by taking too much of a substance. Once they get to this point, it is too painful to stop on their own and too dangerous to continue.

The physical sensations a person experiences during a trauma may continue to afflict the person in future stressful situations. For example, if you experienced a crippling stomachache while you watched your house burn down, you are likely to suffer similar stomachaches each time you face stress. If you woke up with a headache after a tornado ravaged your neighborhood, you might find yourself getting headaches under stressful conditions. These physical symptoms that flare up after a trauma are called psychophysiologic signs.

Finally, people who suffer from PTSD can lose their will to live. If they have been severely traumatized, the victims may come to believe that they have no control over their lives. Feeling out of control can cause hopelessness about the future. They may say to themselves, "Why should I work hard and have hope for the future when I have no control over what happens in my life?" This kind of despair could even lead to suicide.

Consequences of PTSD for Family and Friends

PTSD has the greatest impact on relationships. It is hard to maintain a relationship with a traumatized person. Victims either cling tenaciously to their loved ones, fearing they will lose them, or else purposefully push the loved ones away because they feel that they have not lived up to expectations or provided adequate protection and affection.

Some people find themselves reconnecting with lost family members after a tragedy, but others get caught up in their anger. They blame survivors for surviving; they hold rescuers accountable for the tragedy itself. Friends of victims need to be prepared to prove their loyalty and love over and over again to the trauma victim. The victim no longer believes he has any control over his life. He makes up for this realization by either controlling everyone around him or by withdrawing. He may feel that he cannot trust anyone in the world. As a result, the victim brings bitterness and disillusionment to all of his relationships.

If traumatized individuals turn to alcohol or drugs to numb their pain, they lessen their ability to interact well with others. Aside from the physical health problems they suffer because of the abuse, they will have shortened attention spans, emotional numbing, and an even stronger urge to be "on guard." Worse, if they have problems regulating their emotions in the first place, alcohol will only lessen their inhibitions even more. Contrary to the image of the happy drunk, the traumatized individual who is also a substance abuser will be more irritable and likely to act out his anger aggressively.

Additionally, the substance abuser can become a source of embarrassment to the family. Sharon was in the midst of celebrating her eighth birthday with about twelve of her girlfriends when her mother, who was hosting the party for her (and who was addicted to prescription pain relievers), went into convulsions from an accidental overdose. The horrified children did not know what was happening; everyone thought Sharon's mother was dying. Sharon was scared but also angry that her mother was ruining her party. Once emergency vehicles arrived and took her mother out on a stretcher, the party was over. Sharon later felt guilty for feeling such anger when her mother might have been dying. And that made her angry all over again. Her mother had no right to desert her when she was only eight years old.

Some victims even turn against their loved ones, especially if the disaster resulted in a child's death or injury. Each blames the other because there is no satisfaction in cursing an act of nature. In a way, guilt serves a purpose because it makes the victim believe she really did have some control over the event. If only they had turned on the radio, they would have known a tornado was coming. If only they had made a plan of action in case of fire, they would have all gotten out safely. Blaming yourself and others will not help the situation; it will make matters worse by tearing apart good and loving relationships. It is better to realize that you have little control over external events and begin rebuilding your life.

Abuse: When People Hurt Others

People suffer trauma even at the hands of those they love. Nancy was less than three years old when her father began molesting her. At least, that is as far back as she can actually recall, although it is possible that she was first molested even earlier.

Nancy was born into a wealthy home. When she was two and a half years old, her sister, Kathleen, was born with severe health problems. Both Nancy and her father lost important contact with her mother. Her mother became so absorbed in the care of this younger sister that Nancy became her father's companion.

Nancy had all kinds of feelings about her early childhood. She missed her mother and was jealous of the attention her baby sister got. At the same time, she felt privileged to go everywhere with Daddy because people liked him so much. Daddy told her they had a special relationship, and she wanted to believe that because her mother certainly did not seem to notice her. But she also felt odd, too, because Daddy wanted to do some things with her that did not feel right. In fact, sometimes he hurt her, though he said it would not hurt. He stuck pencils inside her "down there," and he unzipped his pants and rubbed himself against her. He acted strange, too, when he was doing those things, breathing hard, his eyes all glassy. Nancy felt bad whenever he did that. No one ever told her that this kind of behavior was wrong, but her gut told her it was. She never told Mama; she felt that telling on Daddy would bring disaster to her and to their family.

As Nancy grew older, she accepted the touching without complaint. She didn't know it at the time, but she was "numbing out." At night when he stole into her room, she would pretend to be asleep. Daddy fondled her anyway, as she lay there not moving and trying not to notice. "Where is Mama, anyway?" Nancy thought. "She has to know Daddy is doing this."

Nancy tried hard not to become sick, for when she was sick and had to stay home from school, Daddy stayed home with her. Mama was too busy with Kathleen and her doctor's appointments. Nancy was Daddy's problem. On days that she stayed home, and despite her being sick, Daddy still came into her room to touch her.

Sometimes Nancy wished he would do these things to her sister, not her. But then she worried she would lose their special relationship. Her relationship with him—the most powerful man in the world to her—must be preserved at all costs. She continued to submit no matter when or where he wanted to touch her.

She always held out hope that God would save her. Surely if she was a good girl, He would intervene and make her Daddy act like other kids' daddies. God never did. Even when Nancy joined the church; even when she got all A's on her report card; even when she did all her chores without being asked; even then, God did not save her. God had turned his back on her, she reasoned. She must be a very bad person.

Over the years, as the touching turned into actual intercourse, Nancy never said no to her father. She was afraid of his reaction; what if he got angry? He was the only one in her family who was allowed to get angry. He could throw a fit whenever he wished, but anyone else would be punished for such behavior. Nancy had never learned to say no. She didn't know how. She was bitterly angry with both her parents—Dad for abusing her, and Mama for abandoning her. At the same time, she loved them dearly and needed them to survive. She couldn't risk rocking the boat. She needed them.

All these contradictory feelings took their toll. The only way Nancy could survive was to shut down her feelings. She grew increasingly numb, and when it was too hard to act numb, she turned to drugs and alcohol to sedate her awful feelings. She took more and more pills; she drank more and more. She got married and had a little girl, but did not live "happily ever after." Instead, Nancy suffered nightmares, flashbacks, and constricted feelings. In addition, she was severely addicted to prescription pills and alcohol. Nancy was Sharon's mother, the woman discussed earlier who went into convulsions while hosting Sharon's eighth birthday party.

Jayde's Story

Jayde was out with friends celebrating her twenty-first birthday. Since she was now old enough to drink, she went to a local nightclub to celebrate. Her two girlfriends wandered off to find dance partners, while Jayde enjoyed her mixed drinks. Spotting a guy she knew in high school, Jayde called him over to her table to join her. "It's my birthday," she said, making room for him at the table. Spencer smiled. "I guess you're twenty-one now," he said. They drank several more drinks, and though Jayde did not think she had had that much to drink, she suddenly felt dizzy and sick.

She staggered to the bathroom, and Spencer called her friends over. "I think you should take her to the car," he said. "She's pretty drunk. Let her sleep it off."

Ann worried. "Maybe we should take her home."

"And let her folks see her drunk? I don't know about you, but I don't want to be around when her dad finds her in this condition," the other girl said. The two girls and Spencer helped Jayde to the car. Then they went back to the nightclub.

Spencer volunteered to check on Jayde about twenty minutes later. When he got to the car, he slid into the backseat with Jayde and started to undress her. Jayde roused slightly and protested, but Spencer placed his mouth over hers, kissing her to keep her quiet. He continued to peel off her clothes. Jayde passed out again.

When Spencer hadn't returned, Jayde's two girlfriends decided to go looking for him in the parking lot. Maybe Jayde was sicker than they thought. Arriving at their car, they caught Spencer, in a disheveled state, climbing out of the backseat. He turned and ran when he saw them. Jayde lay in the backseat, half awake, with her pants down around her ankles.

The girls took Jayde to the emergency room, where doctors discovered she had alcohol poisoning. Her parents rushed over when called, and Jayde cried when her mother calmed her by saying, "I'm just glad you're alive."

Jayde survived this rape, but she began abusing alcohol, mostly to numb her feelings of guilt and shame. She blamed herself for the rape, and the thing that anguished her most was not knowing if she had encouraged Spencer. In the courtroom, he claimed that Jayde had undressed him as well, and that she had "encouraged him." Although he was ultimately charged with rape, Jayde tortured herself trying to recall what her behavior had been like during the rape. She had been a virgin. Was she still? She would never remember what she had done because the alcohol erased her memories of that night. She finally sought therapy in order to find some peace.

Rape is a life-threatening event. Because the victim thinks that she or he is going to die, or feels humiliated enough to want to die, she or he experiences the same type of symptoms as the combat veteran suffering from PTSD. A survivor can be forever on alert for danger and may lose faith in the basic goodness of the world. She or he may start avoiding certain places and certain people and gradually start to feel constricted and numb.

A single-event trauma is usually recalled vividly. In times of stress, the brain automatically imprints and stores a frightening memory. The memory does not change with time.

Repeated trauma is different. People who have been chronically traumatized (physically or sexually abused over a period of time) repress more of their experiences. They have to deaden themselves to their feelings of rage, helplessness, and shame or they would not be able to survive. Once abuse becomes a pattern, victims usually know when it is coming, and they use tricks to persuade themselves that it is not happening or that it is not that bad. To make matters worse, the perpetrators of these crimes confuse their victims by convincing them that they are acting out of love and concern. One client confessed that her parents would come home drunk several nights a week and her stepfather would molest her, explaining that this was how parents taught their kids about sex. Physically abusive parents try to convince their children that they deserve this mistreatment. Children, who desperately want to love and be loved, eventually believe that they are at fault and deserve what they get. This makes it more difficult for them to try to stop the abuse. Instead of questioning the adults, they question themselves.

Remember: The most severe cases of PTSD result from chronic abuse, especially when it is perpetrated intentionally by a loved one upon whom the child depends.

A Word About Memories

Before we look at why repeated trauma is different from single-event trauma, let's look at how memories are formed and kept. Remembering information has three parts. First, you must perceive something happening. (If people can convince themselves that something is not significant, the brain will not remember it.) Second, the brain stores the information in a variety of places. The more places the information is stored (different sensations are stored in different parts of the brain), the more likely it will be retained. Finally, the brain has to retrieve the information.

When something profoundly shocking happens, we usually recall it without even trying. Can you remember where you were when you heard about the attacks on the World Trade Center and the Pentagon? You may never forget where you were or what you were doing when you heard the news. Our sense of position (where we were at any given time) is particularly keen in an automatic memory. Just as television gives us instant replays, our minds do the same with traumatic memories, until we cannot seem to get the images out of our heads. Of course, the more you rehearse a memory (think about it or talk about it), the more securely it gets stored.

Have you ever awakened from a disturbing dream and immediately told someone about it? The next day, that dream was easier to recall because you had already "rehearsed" it by talking about it. If you wake up, note the dream, but then fall back asleep, chances are you will not recall many details in the morning. That is because the dream was not rehearsed. The same thing applies to studying. The subjects you study the hardest before a test are usually the ones you remember the best. The material you forget to go over ahead of time is usually the hardest to recall.

With a single-event trauma, the memory recalls the event over and over. A repeated trauma is different, though. A child could not survive replaying every instance of repeated physical and sexual abuse, particularly if it came at the hands of a loved one. If a child is abused by a parent, whom can he turn to for support? If his parent treats him like this, who will love him? A child has no one else and no other resources. He cannot live with the memory of these experiences, particularly when they are ongoing. He has to turn his memory off.

How do you stop the memories? Some people simply stop thinking about them. Suppression is the conscious act of not thinking about something. People may run away from their feelings and thoughts but know the bad feelings are still there. You certainly remember that you flunked a math test, but you choose not to think about it.

Repression is different. The person does not do this consciously; he simply stops rehearsing the memory, and as a result, it is not easily recalled. Or he denies reality by thinking, "This isn't happening." If the person does not perceive something happening, it will not be significant enough to be remembered. And if he works hard enough initially to cast the thought aside, he soon "forgets" that it ever happened.

Suppressed and repressed memories are still there, though, and when tapped into, they can usually be recovered in full. Children choose other ways, however, to lose their memories. Rather than resorting to suppression or repression, they often enter trancelike states. At the time something very painful is happening to a child, he or she will enter another world where the pain does not exist. Some chronically abused kids count the dots on ceiling tiles while they are being abused. Other children repeat certain phrases over and over, such as "I'm OK, I'm OK," as a parent advances to hit them. This coping mechanism—this escape from immediate reality to some imaginary safe place in the mind—is known as dissociation.

It is not uncommon for people, especially children, to dissociate in order to survive unthinkable events. Some children dissociate by going someplace in their minds when confronted with stressful events. It allows them to tolerate those events. Some are able to easily pull themselves back to reality when needed. These individuals do not dissociate into separate personalities. Those on the extreme end of the dissociative continuum may hide from severe trauma by allowing their personality to split into several autonomous fragments. People do not consciously choose to enter a dissociative state. It is a coping mechanism that kicks in in extreme cases, and it is not under the person's control.

While dissociative states are helpful because they keep the person unaware of the trauma, they can be dangerous. Pain serves a purpose. It tells us something is wrong and needs to be fixed. If you learn to ignore the pain, you do not do anything positive to end it. If your mind goes somewhere else when you are being abused, you are still being abused. While you may be less aware of it, the trauma still continues.

It takes a bit of effort to dissociate in the beginning, but eventually, it becomes almost automatic. Memories are still stored, but in fragments. Sometimes the brain retains most of the memory but loses the worst or most conflicted part. Many who claim not to remember certain parts of their childhood may have used dissociation in the past to cope. Unfortunately, children who go into trances to avoid pain may discover that they lose their ability to tolerate any strong emotion. They may end up being "emotionless" kids.

The most extreme practitioner of dissociation is the victim of dissociative identity disorder (DID). This is an extremely rare disorder that is thought to affect only 1 percent of PTSD sufferers. Only a highly trained professional can recognize and diagnose it. It should not be confused with the perfectly normal mood shifts of adolescence or the alternating anger, sadness, and fear of PTSD. A person with DID splits off into entirely separate people—not just different personalities—when he or she dissociates. These separate people, called alters, protect him or her from the chronic trauma (usually sexual abuse). The danger is that the original person gets lost among the alters, losing the capacity to integrate the alters' knowledge, emotions, and memories.

People diagnosed with DID have two or more alters, or parts of their personalities, who act like separate individuals. Each has a different style of behavior, different mannerisms, and different speech patterns. Some can even be sick (running fevers) at the same time that other alters are not. Initially, the "host personality" is unaware of these other people. All she may know is that she is missing blocks of time. Her friends may think that these different personalities are really her, but she will not be able to remember doing the things they attribute to her.

Marky is an unusual young woman, and although her story may sound unbelievable, it is entirely true. Marky was severely sexually abused and tortured throughout her childhood. On the dissociative continuum, Marky represents the most extreme. She has what were once called multiple personalities. These separate personae have kept Marky alive. After eight years of therapy, Marky has discovered she has sixty-three alters, or fragments of personalities. She calls them—and herself—"the system."

Marky comes across as a normal, likable young woman. Many are not aware of her dysfunction unless they actually encounter her different alters. As many as 98 percent of the people who develop DID have endured significant childhood trauma, usually before the age of nine. The traumas were usually ongoing, life-threatening, and overwhelming. That is certainly true for Marky. Statistics suggest that DID may occur within 1 percent of the population worldwide, and of people hospitalized for a mental illness, DID accounts for 5 to 20 percent of the patients.

In Marky's case, she has remarkably different and distinct alters. Marky is what is called the host. She is the personality that houses all the rest, and in the beginning, she was unaware she had sixty-three other personalities that frequently took over her body and consciousness. Marky is the person the public sees. There is nothing unusual in her presentation to others; she seems like any other young woman. She appears self-confident, and most people do not know that she is constantly second-guessing herself. She watches people closely for signs of approval or disapproval, and she becomes quite anxious if she senses disapproval. She worries frequently about others; she puts herself last.

Sara, one of Marky's alters, is a five-year-old girl with a very cheerful disposition. She speaks in a child's voice and acts like any other girl her age. She is very friendly and generally trusting of others. She is a soothing presence to Marky and, as such, her purpose is to show up when Marky is in a state of distress. She represents all that is innocent for Marky's system of alters, as Sara never suffered the abuse Marky did. She likes to color, and she is thrilled with the holidays and stuffed animals like Winnie the Pooh and rabbits.

Miss Ruth is an older woman who is the caretaker of the children and other members of this system. She sings to them and holds and rocks them when they are distressed. She also has a calming presence. Whenever

Miss Ruth speaks to others, she always keeps her eyes closed. Miss Ruth is of a different race than the others. Marky knows this because the other alters have told her, and because she can visualize her.

Jo is an outspoken teenager, age sixteen. She's one of the more enjoyable alters because she is both respectful and sassy, appealing to teens and adults alike. She likes fast cars and loud music. She wears dark sunglasses and likes to party. When referring to other alters in Marky's system, she gives them funny nicknames. She is direct at times and occasionally aggressive. Obviously her purpose is to help Marky stick up for herself, as Marky will never say many of the things Jo does. In fact, Jo considers Marky somewhat of a "goody-goody."

It may sound as if Marky has a great way of coping. When she cannot handle the present moment, someone else more capable can step in. That certainly seems like a creative way of dealing with stress.

So why does DID cause problems for Marky? Her symptoms include switching—going from one personality to another (often without any warning for Marky, who enters a sleeplike state when they appear). All sorts of experiences can trigger these switches. When Marky is in public, switching will naturally bring unwanted attention to her. It is also very disorienting, as the personality that switches in may be confused and unaware of what is going on or where she is at that moment. All this switching and hypervigilance makes it impossible for Marky to hold down a steady job.

How Memories Return

Traumatic memories do not deteriorate very much, even if they are repressed or not consciously thought about. A person can live a number of years without being bothered by the traumatic event, but the traumatic memories are stored away nevertheless and can reemerge at any moment.

The structure of the brain has something to do with memory storage. The human brain has four lobes on each side, and each of the lobes has different functions. Long-term memory is located in one place, memory for spatial relationships and physical sensations is located in another, and visual memories and emotions are located in yet another area. Because memories are stored in more than one place, they are particularly resistant to being totally erased. They can be recovered in different ways, depending on what sense you tap into.

Visual cues are the quickest way to retrieve a memory. Seeing something might trigger a memory of something you thought you had forgotten long ago. Sometimes parenting a child who is the same age as you were when the trauma happened will cause a memory to surface. Other times, being in the same place where the trauma occurred will bring the memory back.

Memory is reconstructive, though. That means the memory can change over time, as the individual incorporates other memories into it. Memory changes as we grow older, and our concept of what actually happened, is influenced by what others have said about it. Scientists have shown that chronically abused people have smaller hippocampuses—that part of the brain that forms and holds memories. Additionally, they discovered people with PTSD have higher levels of adrenaline, which keeps the body in a constant state of stress or hyperarousal. These chemicals (cortisol as well as adrenaline) actually eat away at the hippocampus, causing PTSD sufferers to have inaccurate memories.

There are two kinds of memories: implicit and explicit. Explicit memories are also called declarative memories and reflect your ability to remember facts, such as when the Civil War ended and why. Implicit memories are called sensorimotor memories or procedural memories—the way you can recall how to tie your shoes or how to get home from school each day. In the absence of explicit memories, you might not recall how you learned to do something. You just "know."

Traumatized people store their memories in the emotional part of their brains. So when these people remember an event, they will likely recall the feelings and sensations, but not have the language to describe the event or explain what happened. That is because their implicit and explicit memories are separate. In addition, people may have accurate recall of the feelings experienced but not necessarily accurate recall of the facts. The details can deteriorate over time because the brain chemical cortisol is responsible for erasing details in the explicit memories. Since people suffering from PTSD have abnormally low levels of cortisol, it is believed that they have exhausted their supply by previously flooding their brains with cortisol under stress.

The False Memory Debate

What about people who remember things that their families say never occurred? Can therapists plant false memories in their clients? The people who support the idea of false memory syndrome accuse therapists of influencing their clients to recall things that they (the therapists) think might have happened. They suggest ideas, and the client searches his or her memory, certain it must be in there somewhere. Sometimes the client manufactures a memory to please the therapist and to better explain why he or she feels a certain way.

People with more moderate views on the issue agree that memories can be manufactured in the therapist's office (and that is why they discourage hypnosis or asking leading questions of the client), but they believe the overall feelings the client presents are accurate. The implicit recall is not changed much because it is located in the limbic part of the brain. The explicit memory has deteriorated as a result of chemical changes in the brain (specifically the hippocampus where explicit memory is kept) resulting from repeated trauma. Thus the client may recall being fondled but not necessarily by whom.

Therapists opposed to the false memory syndrome believe that repressed memories can return many years later, representing an accurate rendering of the actual event. Because of a better understanding of how the brain and brain chemicals work, many therapists now take the moderate view—that memories aren't always entirely accurate but that they are never totally made up when the client is suffering from PTSD.

When people dissociate, their trancelike states do not allow detailed memories to form. Nevertheless, memories still form, even if they are hazy and fragmentary. Sometimes, only the memory of the "feelings" is stored, while the event itself is not. People have to trust their feelings when trying to figure out if a returning memory is true or not.

Consequences of PTSD for an Abuse Victim

The victim of physical and sexual trauma experiences the same symptoms of PTSD as the victim of a disaster. He is helpless, angry, anxious, and alert to danger around every corner. The victim of repeated abuse experiences more of these symptoms as he starts to recall his traumas.

The victim of sexual abuse often feels an enormous amount of humiliation. She sees herself as dirty and frequently has sleep disorders—either insomnia or nightmares. If the abuse took place during the night, the victim may have trouble getting to sleep and staying asleep, even if she cannot recall the abuse. Her body remembers what happened even if she dissociates from the trauma, and it knows that night is a dangerous time.

Victims of chronic sexual abuse have trouble regulating their emotions and moods. They may struggle with persistent suicidal thoughts; they may cut themselves; they may be prone to explosive outbursts of anger. In addition, they typically feel unlike everyone else. They find themselves unworthy and incompetent; they're filled with shame and self-blame, just like Nancy, who had internalized her father's shame as her own. Many sexually abused children have a profound sense of hopelessness and despair, feeling abandoned by everyone. These feelings combine to make them uncomfortable being around other people who they feel are always judging them. So they isolate themselves and obsess over their shame and perceived shortcomings.

People who try to bury their traumatic memories often become substance abusers because drugs and alcohol can numb the pain. Unfortunately, substance abuse creates additional problems. Both Nancy and Jayde developed significant secondary problems because of their substance abuse. Nancy had to resort to illegal means to maintain her prescription pill addiction, so she was constantly afraid of arrest. She missed out on her daughter's childhood because she was mainly focused on numbing her emotional pain with pills and alcohol. Her relationship with family, especially her daughter, withered because of her embarrassing behavior when under the influence. Jayde became an alcoholic in her efforts to erase the memory of getting drunk and raped. She ultimately attempted suicide when her alcoholism led to increasing irritability and fueled her angry outbursts, driving people she loved away from her.

People who dissociate in order to cope with repeated trauma risk losing themselves. Some children physically hurt themselves to aid the dissociative process or to bring themselves back from a trance by carving on their arms, burning themselves with cigarettes, or sticking themselves with sharp instruments. This self-mutilating behavior becomes a coping mechanism.

People with DID have turbulent lives. They lose blocks of time (when their different alters take over their bodies) and may often engage in self-destructive behavior. Different alters may seek to reenact the sexual trauma by becoming promiscuous. Other alters may want to get rid of the host, believing her to be too weak to function in their best interest.

…equences of PTSD for the Family … Friends of an Abuse Victim

Victims of prolonged abuse understandably have trouble with relationships. They have a tendency to trust too much or too little. The psychologist Erik Erikson noted that a person must negotiate several developmental milestones on his or her way to adulthood. The first task for the child is learning to trust. Understandably, the abused child may never master this developmental task. The child who fails to develop trust tends to bestow it haphazardly on others and ends up being hurt.

The abused child likewise may never master the developmental tasks of initiative and competence. If he has been abused, whether physically or sexually, he may learn not to trust his environment and not to do things for himself because he feels inept. If you see yourself as incompetent, you have to depend on others for the rest of your life. And if you do not trust anyone, you are going to be miserable needing people you cannot trust.

Abuse victims cannot trust others not to hurt them, and that includes loved ones. It is hard for them to relax in any relationship. They perceive sexual threats even when none exist or they sexualize relationships simply because that is how they have grown up relating to people.

As a result, chronically traumatized people have boundary problems with others. They tend to see others as either all good or all bad. They see everyone as a potential rescuer, and they are inevitably disappointed. This may go back to the way they felt about the people in their lives who did not put a stop to their abuse or did not stop it soon enough.

Idolizing someone one minute and then despising him or her the next usually occurs when people fail to live up to the expectations of trauma victims. But it is hard to correct this behavior because trauma victims have trouble seeing both the good and the bad in one person. People with boundary problems (expecting too much from a person) scare off a lot of people with their intense feelings. They are also prone to having trouble expressing their sexual needs appropriately, usually because they never learned how to conduct themselves in a healthy relationship. They have no experience on which to draw.

People who have been raped may have a great deal of trouble engaging in sex again. Even though they may choose a partner and consent to sex in the future, the act of intercourse is often reminiscent of the trauma.

Chronically abused trauma victims have a tendency to reenact their traumas by getting into unstable relationships or by taking care of their abuser later in life. One of my former clients had her stepfather move in with her when her mother died. She claimed he had nowhere else to go and she felt sorry for him. This man had sexually abused her and was a verbally abusive alcoholic. Margaret housed, fed, and humored her stepfather until he died. She never could explain why. She simply had a need to stay connected to this man, even though he had been abusive to her in the past.

Finally, as strange as this may seem, the abuse victim often has conflicted feelings about her abuser, especially if it is her father or another significant person she was dependent upon as a child. No matter what he has done, no matter how degrading or mean-spirited, she still loves him and hopes he will magically turn into the father/stepfather/brother that she always wanted. She may therefore give conflicting messages to her loved ones: despising her perpetrator one minute and defending him the next. The tie may be a toxic one, but it is a significant tie nonetheless.

Witnessing Killing and Kidnapping

Perhaps you have a grandparent, parent, or other relative who served in the Vietnam War. Many Vietnam veterans suffered from PTSD. Their horrible experiences during the fighting were compounded by the strong opposition to the war voiced by many American citizens. Many veterans were reluctant to talk about their experiences. They worked hard to forget what had happened to them over there; as a result many became substance abusers, having started their abuse during the war.

Combat soldiers face death every moment of their tour of duty. They may become dehumanized by all of the killing. The adrenaline rush a soldier experiences during war is hard to turn off, even when he safely returns home. Remember, he has lived with the threat of being tortured and killed for the duration of his service. Many veterans suffer flashbacks and still see danger lurking around every corner. One veteran recalls thinking that little kids shooting off firecrackers on July 4 were snipers on rooftops.

Soldiers are not the only ones to experience the kind of prolonged anxiety and constant threat of death associated with armed combat. Captives—such as prisoners of war, hostages, and kidnapping victims—suffer from the same symptoms of hyperarousal, intrusion, and constriction as anyone else experiencing PTSD as a result of their traumatic experiences.

Associated Press journalist Terry Anderson was the longest-held American hostage in the Middle East. He was captured by Muslim extremists in March 1985 and not released until December 1991, a total of 2,454 days of near total isolation and deprivation. Anderson was chained to a wall during most of his captivity; was fed a meager diet of bread, cheese, and rice; was beaten, taunted, and humiliated; was regularly threatened with death; heard his fellow captives beaten and one die; and grew so depressed he banged his head against a wall until he bled. At times, his captors would isolate him; they would take away his radio, cutting him off entirely from the outside world. He was allowed to use the bathroom only once a day (at their whim, not his need) and a bottle the rest of the time. He wasn't permitted to bathe regularly or wear clean clothes. These conditions were meant to rob him of his dignity.

Fortunately, Terry Anderson retained his dignity by resisting in small ways and discovering a renewed sense of spirituality. This is not to say he did not have his share of terrifying moments, rage, and utter despair, but somehow he maintained reasonably good mental health throughout his ordeal, and he emerged from captivity with a remarkably positive outlook. In a 1996 interview with CNN, Anderson, who now teaches journalism at

Columbia University, said he doesn't resent those years, or the people who took them from him. "People call me a victim of Lebanon, say I lost seven years of my life. I didn't lose them—I lived them . . . Wasted empty years? Not quite. No years are empty in a life. And wasted? That depends on what's made of them after."

Another hostage held by Anderson's captors, Terry Waite, an adviser to the Anglican Archbishop of Canterbury, remained in isolation most of his five years in captivity. (Ironically, he was taken hostage while negotiating for the release of the other hostages in Lebanon, including Anderson.) Nevertheless, he too resisted becoming broken by traumatic stress.

Early in his captivity, he determined that he would not indulge any self-pity. Although at times he was afraid and felt isolated, he maintained hope because, he reasoned, although his captors might have his body and mind, they never would possess his soul. During his captivity, which lasted 1,763 days, he wrote his autobiography in his mind and remembered excerpts from books, poems, and prayers he had memorized as a child. He did not dissociate from the trauma by dividing his self into distinct personalities, nor did he deny the reality of his situation or escape into an imaginary safe place. Rather, he kept a corner of his self private and safe from his captors. They could seize and break everything else, but his soul would be ever beyond their reach.

Today Waite continues to negotiate for the release of hostages in places like Colombia, despite the danger and the traumatic memories associated with this work. He is a testament to a person's ability to heal himself and conquer PTSD by dealing with the trauma head on.

How PTSD Affects the Person

Captives and veterans suffer the same symptoms of hyperarousal, intrusion, and constriction as anyone else experiencing PTSD. With combat or other veterans, the most talked-about symptoms are flashbacks. Most vets don't want to remember their friends' deaths or the enemy soldiers they killed. They need to forget these experiences, but the mind has already stored the memories. While they consciously suppress the material, the memories surface in the form of flashbacks and nightmares. The trauma is too great to file quietly in the back of one's mind. When something evokes the memory, such as a visual cue or a certain smell, the trauma seems to come flooding back and is usually much more than the victim can handle at one moment.

Children who have been kidnapped replay the events in their minds. They also prefer to think that they were in control of the situation as it makes them less vulnerable that way. While children can recall their traumas vividly, they tend to distort time. Unaware of what they are doing, they rethink the trauma and insert things beforehand that really happened after the trauma. Then, based on this scrambled chronology, they actually believe that their trauma was forecast in some way; they just didn't pay attention to the warnings. This makes them feel that they could have had more control over the event.

A person's sense of time is distorted when recalling a traumatic event. Lengthy events seem shorter; short, scary events seem longer. You have probably noticed that boring or scary events seem to last forever, while happier times fly by. It is the same with trauma. A single, scary moment is prolonged because the victim has no idea when it is going to end.

The opposite happens during prolonged trauma. Captives are usually surprised to find that more time has gone by than they think. This is another trick of the mind. If people were truly aware of every second ticking past, they would lose hope in rescue. People without hope lose their will to live; thus, this shortening of time increases the chance of victims being able to "hang in there." They simply have no idea how long they have been traumatized.

Consequences of PTSD for Former Hostages and Veterans

Former hostages startle more easily than other people, and they acquire anxieties often associated with childhood, such as fears of the dark, strangers, loud noises, or deep water. Unlike children, however, they may have trouble "outgrowing" their fears. Even though they were not traumatized in the dark, veterans and former captives may now be afraid of the dark. They simply develop ordinary fears after having experienced a trauma and react strongly to these feelings.

Hostages, including combat veterans who are in a sense hostages to the war, experience shame, guilt, and helplessness. That is exactly what captors want their victims to feel because they know these emotions break the hostages' will to resist. Victims feel especially degraded and often lose hope when they have been forced to commit atrocities or hurt others to save themselves. These people have no sense of a future; they don't care about living a long life because they cannot envision surviving a long time with these memories. Children may give up on their goals and behave self-destructively, or they may take up a risky hobby, such as motorcycle racing or skydiving. Some start hanging out with a rough crowd. Young women may drop out of school to get married at an unusually early age.

Many hostages develop substance abuse problems (as do combat veterans) because it seems like a quick fix to obliterate the pain. Most do not drink to relax; they drink to forget what has happened to them. Teenagers do not necessarily turn into alcoholics right after a trauma, but they are more likely to experiment with drugs as a way to avoid their feelings. They may eventually turn to alcohol, simply because it is a more socially acceptable way to escape problems in this society than is drug use. Many people still do not consider alcohol a drug.

Some people develop other psychological disorders under the stress of prolonged captivity, including paranoia and delusions. Some people manage to continue living a regular life despite problems with irritability, paranoia, anxiety, and/or depression. There are degrees to all these symptoms. Some people can get along being a little paranoid, particularly if their loved ones understand and tolerate it. But delusions (thinking things that are not real) and hallucinations (seeing or hearing things that are not actually there) are more serious manifestations of prolonged stress.

Consequences of PTSD for Family and Friends of Former Hostages and Veterans

Hostages and combat veterans alike have a great deal of anger, and it is usually misdirected. Vietnam War soldiers were mad at the enemy, but in most cases, the enemy was invisible, or seemed to be, and was always out of reach. Unfortunately, others were always around to catch the brunt of the soldiers' anger, and it was not usually deserved.

Tim O'Brien, a writer and Vietnam veteran, tells the story of a soldier who was wounded in combat. Having been shot and in danger of bleeding to death, the man screamed for a medic. Unfortunately, the medic was new to combat and momentarily froze with fear. The soldier kept screaming, but the medic did not come. Eventually—and in reality, it probably was not so very long—the medic reached the soldier who was by then going into shock.

The soldier recovered but suffered for a long time afterward with infections from the gun wound on his buttocks. He could not sit and had to apply special ointment every few hours to the wound. The soldier was temporarily moved to an office job, which at first was great, until he realized that he was no longer "one of the guys." His combat buddies had bonded with the medic, the very man who had let him go into shock.

The soldier burned with anger and kept thinking of ways to get even. All his rage was aimed at the medic, although the enemy had shot him, and the medic was simply a rescuer who had not gotten to him in time to prevent shock. Unable to vent his anger on the real enemy, the soldier took it out on the rescuer. This often happens with kidnapping victims. They end up more angry at those who were not able to rescue them in time to spare them the trauma than with their attackers.

Soldiers have special problems because they feel reluctant to unburden themselves in therapy. They are hesitant to share their secrets, some of which may be classified military information. They are usually quick to defend their governments because their own judgment and actions would be called into question if they attacked the institutions that sponsored them and gave them their orders. Unable to vent their contradictory feelings, they suffer prolonged symptoms of PTSD: hypervigilance (trying to keep the secrets hidden), constriction (avoiding people who might find out too much), and intrusive memories that come back in nightmares and flashbacks.

Trauma victims tend to be cross with their loved ones. While relieved to be reunited with them, a part of them resents having gone through the trauma alone. As with other PTSD victims, they find it hard to trust in a relationship. Loving someone means opening yourself up to the possibility of losing him or her. People who have already faced death and isolation are not always willing to risk loving again. This, of course, makes it doubly hard on the loved one, who has to prove over and over again that he or she will not leave and will not stop loving.

PTSD victims may smother loved ones with their dependence or torment them with their indifference. And they may do both at different times of the day or week. The loved ones, therefore, never know what to expect or how to respond.

Terrorist Attacks, Accidents, and Other Traumatic Situations

On September 11, 2001, several groups of terrorists working together hijacked four commercial jets and attacked the World Trade Center in New York City and the Pentagon in Arlington, Virginia, just across the Potomac River from Washington, D.C. The planes were used as missiles to fly directly into these buildings, and the resulting devastation was almost beyond comprehension. In addition to the severe structural damage inflicted on the Pentagon building and the deaths of some 180 workers, both towers of the World Trade Center collapsed to the ground, resulting in the deaths of almost 5,000 office workers, airline passengers, service workers, and rescue personnel.

As workers rushed down the towers' staircases, firefighters and police officers rushed up them to try to rescue those trapped on the upper floors. Hundreds of these rescuers were lost when the towers collapsed. In the wake of the collapses, as survivors straggled away from the area in a state of shock, hundreds of additional rescue workers and ordinary citizens rushed to the disaster area to offer whatever help they could. Many New Yorkers watched this nightmarish scene unfold from their offices or apartment rooftops. This was not just a local incident, however;

most of America watched the events play out live on television, then watched them replayed endlessly over the following hours and days.

Due to the highly interactive and immediate nature of modern media technology, our satellite broadcasts, Internet access, and rapid-fire e-mails made this perhaps the most communally shared trauma in American history. As a result, nearly all Americans were affected by the shattering images of destruction, death, and grieving broadcast repeatedly and discussed in great detail in the wake of the attacks. Nearly all Americans found themselves troubled by anxiety, anger, sorrow, dread, confusion, and fear since September 11. Because we all witnessed the events as they unfolded, in a sense we were all coping with some of the typical symptoms of PTSD.

Mental health professionals were particularly concerned for the loved ones of those killed, the World Trade Center and Pentagon survivors, and the rescue workers who were on the scene that day and in the days that followed. Hospitals all over New York City staffed walk-in crisis counseling centers for anyone who needed help in coping with what he or she had seen and experienced. Web sites, hotlines, and crisis centers were created especially for police officers, firefighters, and other rescue workers who are often the most vulnerable to developing PTSD in the aftermath of this kind of attack; unfortunately, they are also often the least likely to seek help because of a sense of shame or weakness. Counseling is crucial, however. Without it, many of those directly affected by the attacks may have lost their jobs, their relationships, and even their ability to participate in everyday activities.

Experts believe that those who were at the World Trade Center or Pentagon were the most likely to be haunted by vivid memories of the events, suffer from recurring nightmares or flashbacks, and experience anxiety attacks triggered by certain sounds or smells. Yet even those Americans who experienced the events only by television were not safe from developing PTSD symptoms; we were all confronted with our vulnerability and frailty on that day. Feelings of horror, edginess, anger, and avoidance (such as declining to fly or staying away from cities) are common and perfectly normal reactions to this kind of trauma. The best way to get past this initial reaction is to talk through it with family, friends, and a therapist, if necessary.

A road map to the trauma we may feel and the ways in which we may cope after this kind of violent act has been provided to us by an earlier terrorist attack on American soil. On April 19, 1995, a 4,800-pound bomb tore apart the Alfred P. Murrah Federal Building in downtown Oklahoma City, Oklahoma. At first, people thought international terrorists had struck the heartland of America. Later, law enforcement officials arrested American suspects.

More than 500 people were conducting business in the building that day at 9:00 AM. One young woman had stopped by to get a social security card for her four-month-old son. She brought along her son, her three-year-old daughter, her mother, and her sister; only the woman and her sister survived the explosion.

In addition to the various government offices in the building, there was a day-care center on the second floor. The bomb brought seven floors down on top of the day-care center; few children survived the explosion. Across from the building, glass shards from the explosion rained down on another day-care center. People as far as two blocks away were knocked over by the explosion.

One man who worked in the Murrah building dove under his desk when the bomb exploded. Seconds later he stuck his head out to survey the damage and realized that his desk and the floor space it occupied stood unscathed, while the rest of the floor had been blown away. He looked up at the sky and below to a gaping hole in the center of the building. He was one of the lucky ones; he got out alive. Most victims were buried in concrete and falling debris as the nine stories fell one on top of another.

Rescue workers, as well as survivors in the building, soon began to feel the effects of PTSD. Firefighters, medical doctors, and other rescue personnel from nearby cities converged on Oklahoma City to search for bodies and assist the families of the victims. At first, rescuers were buoyed by finding survivors, but as the hours wore on and bad weather hampered rescue efforts, chances of finding anyone else alive diminished. Rescue personnel were overwhelmed by such massive devastation and death. By the end of the first day, rescuers were finding more bodies than survivors. As fatigue set in, it became harder to shut out their feelings. Many workers went home to their family members and wept.

As the Oklahoma City bombing has shown, the victims were not simply the people who died. The trauma greatly affected the people who survived, and especially the people who tried to rescue those buried alive. Both the survivors and the rescue personnel needed support to handle the tragedy.

While terrorist attacks on American cities are uncommon, many Americans already have firsthand experience with PTSD as a result of dangerous and violent conditions in their neighborhoods and schools. In many places, citizens are warned not to use automated teller machines at banks even in broad daylight because of the risk of robbery. Even children in public schools are not safe from attacks. The 1999 shootings at Columbine High School in Littleton, Colorado, and in Santee, California, in March 2001 show that children do not seem to be safe anywhere. After the shootings in California, my teenage daughter was sitting in her fourth period class at her high school in Oklahoma when an explosion occurred. Students thought a gunman had started shooting in the corridor. They dove under their desks, and the teacher ran to lock their classroom door. It turned out that someone's science experiment had blown up in the lab. Though kids laughed about it later, many had stomachaches the rest of the day. The fact that most students thought they were being attacked illustrates the climate of fear that persists after a traumatic event.

Many people assume that young children have no memory of trauma. According to psychologists, children under the age of twenty-eight months cannot put their thoughts into words. In many cases, they will feel the trauma and store memories of those feelings and sensations, rather than of the actual events. Little children still react to the trauma, though. They fear trauma-related stimuli—things that remind them of the original trauma—and they reenact the traumas in their play. Most people do not notice, however, because they would not expect such a youngster to recall the trauma.

Potentially traumatic situations are all around, in both the cities and suburbs. Violence in our society has become all too common. Weapons are easily obtained and used for minor grievances, such as disputes over "turf." Kids start to get used to the violence because it surrounds them. People think that means they have adjusted, but really it serves only to harden them. If you live in an environment in which people routinely get shot in their schools, neighborhoods, and homes, you come to accept that kind of behavior as normal. It makes it that much easier for you to do the same thing. Your mind and body have to go on perpetual alert from being around so much danger. You always have to watch your back. That is hyperarousal, one of the three cardinal symptoms of PTSD. Kids who grow up surrounded by violence lose their hope for the future because there is a good chance that they will not stay alive long enough to have much of a future. Finally, they numb themselves to all the violence—in other words, they go through constriction, another sign of PTSD. Drugs and alcohol temporarily help people survive violent environments, but of course, drug and alcohol abuse and addiction only add to the problem.

In addition to school shootings and neighborhood violence, kids may see other horrific acts that they can barely comprehend. Krista was in my fifth grade homeroom. That year, her grandfather died, and her mother slipped into depression. No one knew what was wrong with Krista's mother, except that she never drove Krista to school anymore and she did not come to any of the PTA meetings.

One morning I found my own mother exclaiming over the newspaper. Krista's mother had apparently hanged herself the day before and her body was found by Krista and one of her sisters. Krista never talked about the trauma. Her father had told her, "What's done is done. We can't change it now. I don't want to hear about it anymore." And Krista kept all that horror inside her. Years later she had turned into a sad, timid person who had left school before graduating and had married at seventeen.

Two high school friends were driving home from a football game. They had both been drinking and were exhilarated by their school's win. Just a couple of miles from their neighborhood, Tommy lost control of the car and smashed head-on into a tree on the side of the road. Brandon was not wearing a seat belt and was thrown from the car, dying instantly. Tommy was banged up and bloodied by his airbag, but he was alive. Taken to the emergency room, he was treated and later released. That was only the beginning of his painful recovery, however. Brandon had been his best friend. They were both going to graduate next spring and be roommates in college. Tommy did not want to face Brandon's parents; after all, he had killed his best friend, their son. It was his fault.

Jeannette and her older sister, Kelly, were riding home from the mall. Jeannette pulled up to the four-way intersection. She stopped, waiting her turn to go. She pulled into the intersection, and suddenly—out of nowhere—a truck barreled through the stop sign. It tore into the passenger side of Jeannette's car, killing Kelly. The driver was arrested for driving while intoxicated and charged with manslaughter. Jeannette was taken to the hospital in shock.

The physical scars healed, but the emotional wounds festered for years. Jeannette felt responsible for the accident that claimed her sister's life. Furthermore, she felt if anyone had to die, it should have been her. She had never done well in school, but Kelly had been both popular and an academic star. Kelly had had big plans for a career in Washington as a lobbyist. What plans did Jeannette ever have beyond making a passing grade in a math course and eventually getting out of high school? Jeannette could not be consoled. She should have been the one to die; she hadn't deserved to live in place of Kelly. Every night she replayed driving up to the intersection. Each time she tried to change what happened next, but her mind always replayed the truth, and Kelly was killed over and over again.

Jeannette's reaction to the car accident was by no means unusual or extreme. She suffered from "survivor guilt"—a feeling that she did not deserve to survive and should have been the one to die. This is a common post-traumatic response. Accident statistics show that approximately 9 percent of those people involved in motor vehicle accidents will develop symptoms of PTSD. If someone dies as a result of an accident, the odds increase that the surviving person will develop PTSD. Motor vehicle accidents are one of the most common traumas leading to PTSD.

Witnessing extreme violence, even when your own life is not in danger, is also traumatizing. People who have watched tragedies happen to others usually think, "It could have happened to me." And that is what is so scary. It *could* have happened to you. Life-threatening situations cause trauma, even when they happen to someone else. Witnessing a loved one die is even worse. Some people would prefer to be the victim. Being helpless to save a loved one from tragedy is extremely traumatic. Seeing loved ones killed or injured is more powerful than seeing strangers killed, but witnessing any act of extreme violence can provoke symptoms of PTSD.

Consequences of PTSD for Victims of Violence

Abraham Maslow was a psychologist who devised a "Hierarchy of Needs" to explain how people are motivated. If you think of the hierarchy as a ladder, your basic needs for survival comprise the lower rung. Those are your needs for sustaining life: eating, drinking water, and breathing. Just above those needs is the need for security or freedom from fear; once your basic physiological needs are met, you need shelter and a safe environment. Farther up the ladder comes attachment, the need to love and be loved, and then self-esteem, the need to feel good about yourself.

These basic needs of survival—security, attachment, and self-esteem—are called deficiency needs because Maslow considered a person deficient, or missing something, without any one of them. A person would not be motivated to move on to fulfill his growth needs—things that improve his character and mind—until he had satisfied these primary needs. The growth needs are cognitive (the need to learn new things, not just school subjects), aesthetic (the need for beauty in your environment), self-actualization (living up to one's potential), and transcendence (spiritual needs).

Let's look at the lower part of Maslow's ladder. If a person lives in a violent environment, he is stuck trying to meet his needs for security. He is not motivated to decorate his apartment with beautiful things (aesthetic needs) or take up meditation (transcendence) just yet. The person is concerned about making ends meet or keeping himself from getting shot on the way to the store. Many high school students today are faced with daily acts of violence that were unknown in their parents' generations. Their neighborhoods may be overrun with drugs and gangs. They may endure verbal, physical, or sexual harassment in the hallways. They may also fear that their school could be the next Columbine. Will such environments foster good students? According to Maslow, they will not, given a student's most pressing need is to stay alive (security needs) rather than learn algebra (cognitive needs). In other words, when schools and neighborhoods are dangerous places, not much learning is going to occur. People become chronically stressed and do not think beyond their immediate future (getting home safely that day).

The victim is constantly on the alert, and that takes a toll on his good humor as well as his body. Traumatized people, especially chronically traumatized people, look much older than others their age. Chronic anxiety often wears a body out.

Victims become edgy and irritable over seemingly inconsequential things. They may blow up if you forget to return a pencil you borrowed. They may think you are laughing at them if you smile as they walk by. These are symptoms of paranoia and evidence of the hyperaroused state of a PTSD sufferer. Continually faced with bad memories, victims often get depressed, especially if they cannot reconcile the memories or make them go away. Depression causes a person to cry a lot, to lose hope that she will ever get better, to lose sleep, have no appetite, and lose interest in her appearance. Victims of violence are often afraid to go to sleep—to fall asleep one has to relax. Chronically stressed people and those who have witnessed extreme acts of violence are not initially capable of relaxing. Insomnia—not being able to get a good night's sleep—only compounds the problem because sleep deprivation takes away a person's good judgment and makes him that much more irritable. If someone lives in a frightening environment, it may not be safe to sleep. That person either has to numb himself to the constant threats or live in terror.

A constricted life is filled with losses. If you learn to avoid people, you become subject to loneliness and isolation. If you are afraid to venture out, you may miss out on many community events. If you cannot let yourself love anyone because he or she may be taken from you one day in an act of violence, you have lost the chance to share your life with someone. You will have effectively cut yourself off from all human contact, the very contact you need to cope with PTSD and heal yourself.

Isolating yourself from others contributes to paranoia and a strong sense of abandonment. Just because you are feeling irritable or edgy does not mean you will get better by staying away from people. In the long run, if you employ this coping mechanism, you will feel more alone and misunderstood. Granted, you will not be getting into fights with people if you hide from them, but you cannot hide from your thoughts, your memories, and especially your feelings. And these will follow you everywhere.

Consequences of PTSD for Family and Friends of Victims of Violence

Chronically vigilant people can make mistakes. Sometimes being so alert to possible danger makes you see danger where none exists. Sometimes people overreact in traffic because they assume other people mean to cut them off and intentionally inflict harm. Easily provoked people tend to turn off other people.

Family members and friends may make belated attempts to shield you from further violence, but most victims do not want to be overprotected. People expect others to keep them from harm (which is not entirely possible), and yet people want to go off and do their own thing when the mood strikes. You cannot have it both ways. So victims develop overdependence on loved ones and resent them at the same time.

Some people have an exaggerated need for reassurance and approval following violence-induced trauma. They worry that they might be doing something wrong even when they rationally know they have not done anything. They constantly ask others, "Are you mad at me? Am I in trouble?" Often this kind of paranoia results in others avoiding the victim because they tire of having to reassure him or her everything is okay over and over and over.

Survivors of violence are more prone than the average person to think about ending their lives. They might make attempts, or just talk about it, but the end result is the same for their family members and friends who may feel angry (at being so powerless to stop the victim), guilty (for wanting relief from the constant worrying), and afraid (that they might lose their loved one for good).

If the traumatized victim of violence turns to alcohol or drug abuse, family members experience additional anger, embarrassment, futility, and possible financial ruin. Family members who counsel abstinence cannot easily compete with the false hope and relief that the substances provide the victim. They are justifiably resentful that the victim prefers the substance to their love and support.

Some trauma victims lose their ability to form attachments; it is simply not worth the effort. Loving is too scary. Many victims of violence prefer to look out for themselves. They may seem friendly at times but feel they cannot afford to love and make themselves vulnerable to loss.

Constricted people sometimes restrict not only their own lives but everyone else's as well. Residents of crime-ridden neighborhoods try to keep their children safe by locking them inside. Yet the adult victims still do not feel safe, and their children feel punished for living in an unsafe environment.

Victims of violence also stop trusting people. They believe the world is not a safe place. Cars can crash, mothers hang themselves, and terrorists kill innocent people. As a result of seeing danger everywhere, victims distrust everyone. Friends and relatives probably understand where this distrust comes from but can get tired of the victim's ever-present fear. And accommodating his or her wishes to avoid places or people may cause friction over time.

Part II:
Treatment for PTSD

5 Negative Ways of Coping

Anyone who has ever suffered a traumatic experience has probably found himself or herself using some or all of the following methods to keep the memories at bay. He or she has also probably found that these methods do not work for long but simply create more problems in the end.

Alcohol and Drugs

Alcohol seems to be a good way to numb emotions. You may feel frightened or anxious, so you decide to have a beer or two, and then before you know it, you are not thinking about that problem anymore. If memories stayed away for good, and alcohol did not lead to so many other physical problems, this might be a suitable remedy. But traumatic memories are not dispelled by alcohol. Under the influence you might not feel their impact, but the memories are still there and will continue to haunt you after you sober up. You will have to keep drinking in order to continue keeping the memories at bay.

Contrary to what most people think, alcohol is a depressant, not a stimulant. That means it brings you down; it does not give you energy. Feelings sometimes become exaggerated when combined with alcohol, even as they sometimes seem less significant. You cannot always predict how alcohol will affect your emotional state. Some people become moody and depressed, while others may act silly and inappropriate.

Alcohol abuse ravages your body. It can eventually destroy your liver and can lead to heart complications and addiction. Alcohol abuse ruins families as well. When people depend on alcohol to banish their problems, they often retreat from others. They can become mean, hostile, and uncooperative because alcohol destroys judgment. A person who has had too much to drink lacks the coordination and reaction time necessary to drive a car safely. He or she also lacks the good sense to know when he or she is out of line and behaving inappropriately. A diminished sense of responsibility often leads to poor performance at work and school and poor interactions with others, straining the very relationships that can provide necessary help and support

If poor health and ruined relationships are not enough to turn you off to alcohol, consider this: Alcohol disturbs sleep. Many victims of PTSD are plagued with insomnia and nightmares. Alcohol may initially relax people enough to enable them to fall asleep, but they will sleep fitfully, and their sleep will be light and broken. The nightmares do not necessarily go away, either. In fact, when someone quits drinking, he or she will often have an onslaught of nightmares for the first several nights as part of the withdrawal process.

Drugs function in much the same way that alcohol does. Some may pep you up so that you feel good temporarily, but you will come back down eventually, and the memories will still be there. Other drugs claim to relax you and mellow you out. If that's all that happened, they might be a good alternative to facing your trauma. But that is not all that happens. Depending on which drugs you use and how much, you can ruin your health, your initiative, your relationships, and your brain. Drugs can impair judgment because they disrupt chemical messages in the brain and provoke violent mood swings. Drugs, even prescription drugs, can disrupt sleep patterns, causing insomnia or loss of dream sleep. If all your dreams have been nightmares, you might think that sleeplessness is a good thing. However, a loss of REM sleep—during which dreaming usually occurs—is detrimental to your mental health. REM sleep seems to refresh the mind so that you are able to think more clearly in the morning. Without sufficient REM sleep, your judgment is not as sharp and your mood is not as stable.

Since drugs can be an escape, it is easy to become addicted—especially to the less expensive, faster-acting highs. Drugs can also lead to physical problems, including heart attacks and overdoses. They are also often expensive.

Sexual Acting Out

Some psychologists view sexual acting out as an escape, but most believe it is a reenactment of the original trauma. People who use their bodies promiscuously have often been victims of chronic sexual abuse. They either decide that they are "damaged goods" already and promiscuity does not matter, or they end up reliving what once happened to them.

Adele was sexually abused by her stepfather beginning when she was five. By the time she was in high school, she had earned a reputation among her classmates as being "fast" and "easy" with the guys. Although Adele was ashamed of her promiscuity, she could not bring herself to stop this pattern of behavior. She had learned at an early age that many people related to her in a sexual way, and that was the only way she knew of making and keeping friends.

Eventually Adele ended up in therapy for severe depression. Within a few sessions, she found herself propositioning her male therapist. Even though she needed this man to relate to her on a more professional level, she could not help but try to sexualize this relationship as well. Fortunately, her therapist recognized this behavior as a trauma reenactment and was able to maintain the strict boundaries of their relationship.

Other victims may become so disgusted with themselves that they no longer care what happens to them. Having no belief in a future, they persist in behaviors that might bring them physical satisfaction (initially) or financial gain, but ultimately confirm their low opinion of themselves.

At the same time, sexual acting out is an escape. You cannot dwell on scary memories when you are supposedly having a good time. But the problem remains: Your self-esteem suffers when you realize you have not gotten rid of the memories by acting out and you have risked disease on top of it all.

Leslie had been dating her latest boyfriend, C[illegible] for just a couple of weeks. He was so attractive, and all the girls at school were jealous of her. One afternoon they stopped at Chad's house so he could change his clothes. He invited her in, and she discovered his parents weren't home. He coaxed her into the bedroom. She pretended to resist but followed him in. He pushed her down on the bed, and she laughed, thinking he was teasing her, trying to scare her. Then she realized he was serious; he was tearing her clothes off.

"Hey!" she yelled. "You're ripping my blouse. Stop it!"

He didn't say anything but just kept pulling off her clothes. With one arm, he held her down firmly on the bed. Then he raped her.

Leslie never said a word. Tears streaked her face as she struggled to pull her clothes back on.

Surprisingly, Chad changed his clothes and asked if she was ready to go out and get something to eat.

"Just take me home," Leslie said.

Chad complied.

After getting home, Leslie called her best friend, Bree. She told her what had happened, and Bree expressed her outrage and shock. Leslie only whimpered her agreement.

But at school, Chad acted hurt when Leslie avoided him. "Why are you acting this way after I expressed my love for you?" he asked, sounding truly surprised.

Leslie cringed, "You call that love? You raped me."

"That was not rape," he said. "You never said no. If I remember correctly, you never said anything. Besides, I never hurt you."

Leslie felt guilty. It was true; she hadn't said no. Maybe it wasn't rape after all.

She called Bree after school and told her what Chad had said. Bree again expressed her shock. "That's what you call date rape," she said. "You need to call the police or the rape prevention center."

Leslie didn't want to do that. "It's not a big deal," she said. "He says he loves me, you know."

"I don't care what he says," Bree objected. "That's not love."

"Well, we're going out tonight; I'll talk some more to him about it."

Only she never got to tell Chad how she felt because he protested that she was rejecting him. Leslie began to think she was the one with a problem. She decided not to say anything more; she went on the birth control pill instead and continued to have sex with Chad, although often against her will.

A few months later, Leslie admitted to Bree that she and Chad were going to move in together after they graduated in the spring. Bree rolled her eyes, but she couldn't convince Leslie that she was making a mistake.

Leslie had grown up in a physically abusive home; this kind of abusive behavior was clearly second nature to her. Leslie had not wanted to deal with the rape, so she accepted her boyfriend's claim that it was an act of love. But she still felt used and anguished; she just did not know why.

Suicidal and Self-Destructive Behavior

The inability to imagine a future is a symptom of PTSD. People who no longer care about life may behave recklessly and get killed. One Vietnam veteran began skydiving after his stint in Vietnam. He was not consciously taking up a dangerous sport that could kill him, but he was putting himself at risk every time he jumped out of a plane. The thrill of doing something so dangerous took his mind off his memories of Vietnam—for a while.

Other victims of PTSD may be more direct, purposely setting out to kill themselves in a desperate way to end their suffering. The problem with suicide is that you hurt others, too. If you succeed in taking your life, you will have traumatized those you leave behind. Remember Krista? Not only did Krista's mother leave the family by hanging herself, but she horrified the family when they found her dead. The mother may have escaped her depression, but she passed an even greater horror onto her children.

Suicides do not always succeed. Many victims botch their attempts and in so doing develop other physical problems. Drug overdoses are not always fatal but can ruin your internal organs so that your body deteriorates well before you die. Sometimes you damage your brain so severely that you cannot function anymore, and you are left without the energy or ability to carry out another suicide attempt.

People who attempt suicide may do so because they are tired but cannot sleep long enough or deeply enough to gain any benefits. They don't necessarily mean to die; they just want an escape from their problems and their intrusive memories. Often, they are not thinking rationally because their hope is to reunite with a deceased loved one, or they want to punish others with their death, as if they will be able to watch their own funerals and observe the tormented mourners. Suicide is not the ultimate revenge because you do not live to see the results. Dying is not a way to cope with bad memories.

Some PTSD victims wish to harm themselves but stop short of suicide. People who have numbed themselves to a great trauma in the past find it hard to retrieve their feelings later. They resort to cutting themselves, watching their wounds bleed, and trying to recapture the feeling of pain; the difference is that this time they feel in control of the wounding and the pain.

Sometimes adults and hospital staff mix up an individual's desire to hurt herself with a desire to kill herself. Self-mutilation usually is not a suicide attempt. Many teenagers use cutting to experience physical pain or as a way to bring themselves out of a trance when they've been dissociating (numbing themselves to emotional pain). Sometimes people hurt themselves as a way to prove they are alive. If you make yourself bleed, then you must be alive. These people are not trying to take their lives, although sometimes that can happen accidentally if they are not careful about what they do. As strange as it sounds, this self-mutilation is a coping mechanism to help them bear the pain of past abuse and awful memories. It gives them something else to focus on. Of course, it is not a positive way to cope because of the possibility of severe injury and death.

Losing Your Feelings

Dissociation, or numbness, does serve a purpose to the victim of a trauma. Initially, it allows him or her to go on functioning in the face of extreme terror. When a person is better able to cope, his or her numbness gives way to anger. Anger is a great energizer and gets the victim moving again. But some people get stuck in the numb stage. They do not want to feel the pain and horror all over again, so they keep their feelings under wraps. You can not selectively feel the good stuff and deny the bad. Emotionless people go through life isolated from others and unable to integrate the trauma into their life experience. More important, they miss out on the joyful events that come along.

Researchers have discovered why many people suffering from PTSD exhibit numbing behaviors. People with PTSD release a larger amount of endorphins than people without PTSD. Endorphins are the body's natural painkillers that are released into your bloodstream when you are faced with traumatic circumstances. Their purpose is to numb you to pain in order to help you survive whatever trauma presents itself.

Since people with PTSD have chronically aroused systems, they release endorphins almost constantly. As a result, they become anesthetized to emotional pain as well. These people aren't "numbing out" on purpose; their bodies are simply working overtime to help them cope with a constant state of traumatic stress.

Avoidance of Reminders

In the short term, avoiding reminders of a trauma helps make the memories and feelings tolerable. In the long run, however, the victim is using avoidance to escape working out his or her feelings about the trauma. Memories do not die simply because you are not tapping into them. Eventually they will come back when a new reminder brings them to the surface. In the meantime, you are missing out on things by restricting your life. When you live in fear, even of a memory, you are surrendering to the power of the trauma. There are far better ways to deal with your feelings.

Repressed memories do not go away; they are alive and well inside us. Until you confront the trauma and your feelings surrounding it, you will be subject to repetitive dreams and reenactments, which could set you up for even more abuse.

Children's Reactions to Trauma

Children sometimes react to trauma through rigidity and regression. Rigidity is a form of avoidance. The child has been so shocked by the event or series of events that he withdraws into himself or his home. He may not want to go outside anymore or visit a friend's house. Constricting his life in such a rigid fashion (which is not necessarily a conscious act) is a normal reaction to trauma, but if it continues for a long time, it becomes a negative way of coping. Rigid children grow up to be rigid adults whose emotions are deadened.

Children and teenagers tend to regress in times of stress. That means they revert to behavior more suited to a younger child. If they are traumatized when they are six, they may regress to the behavior of a three-year-old. Any time before the trauma was a safer time, and the child can reduce his anxiety by acting as if he is back in that safer time. Of course, regression does not change anything. You can act younger, but you do not really become younger, and the experiences do not go away. Regression is normal behavior for anyone overwhelmed by trauma, but if it persists too long, it becomes another form of avoidance.

Finally, although it might be normal to try to make some sense out of the trauma, there comes a time when you have to move on. You cannot make sense out of something senseless. Bad things happen in this world. People can drive themselves crazy trying to understand why the awful event happened to them, but usually no rational explanation exists. Spending all of your time figuring out the greater meaning of the event will take time away from your healing.

A Support System

Most important to trauma victims is the knowledge that they are safe. They cannot work on other issues such as anger, sorrow, and grieving until they are certain the immediate environment is secure. Their loved ones, friends, and the larger community can provide that support.

Your Loved Ones

A man was jogging through a park some time ago. For a short stretch, the trail ran alongside a heavily traveled street. As he jogged along this stretch, he saw a carload of men pass by. He heard a loud bang and thought the car had backfired, and then he stumbled. As he tried to regain his footing, he saw the blood on his thigh and realized he had been shot.

His girlfriend found him and rushed him to the hospital. Fortunately the wound was not life threatening, but the man was severely traumatized. Now when he jogs, his girlfriend stays at his side or he goes in a group. His girlfriend's continuing concern for his safety made him feel less traumatized. He was also relieved to see that park officials responded quickly to the shooting by instituting new security features such as increased lighting and the planting of more shrubbery to serve as a barrier between the street and trail.

When a person has suffered a trauma, he or she feels frightened and alone. Loved ones can do two things for the victim: They can provide reassurance of their continuing love at a time when he of she might not be feeling so lovable, and they can stay with the victim to keep him or her safe.

If the victim has been raped, she will feel safer if someone she knows and trusts accompanies her to the hospital and police station. The exam and police questioning can often seem like another violation, and a trusted loved one can help ease the victim's passage through these procedures.

The loved one is not helpful to the victim, however, when he or she overreacts to the situation. He or she does not help the victim feel safe again by taking away her independence. If the loved one expresses all the victim's rage for her, the victim does not learn to express the rage herself. If the loved one restricts the victim's life, the victim never learns to conquer her fears.

After a disaster, loved ones can help by moving victims to safer areas. However, it is important to let the victim make these decisions. He or she needs to be able to decide when to go back and face the fears. Loved ones need to protect, but not constrict.

Trauma victims need their loved ones to listen to them and believe them. Rape and abuse victims often feel guilt over the trauma, as if they had some control over the event. Of course, people never deserve their traumas; these are terrible things that sometimes just happen. The victim needs to talk about the experience to sort out his or her feelings. Some loved ones are so caught up in their own anguish and guilt because they could not prevent the trauma that they cannot stand to hear about the victim's pain.

But that is another thing the victim needs from a loved one: someone to listen without censoring the victim's feelings. The victim does not need to be judged. He or she does not need to be told, "Oh, don't think about that anymore." The feelings do not go away simply because the victim stops talking about them. And crying is not a bad reaction to a trauma. Crying is a normal response to a loss, and any trauma victim has suffered a loss, whether it is virginity, possessions, or a sense of innocence and security. If the victim has no one with whom to share feelings, he or she is likely to bottle them up. Feelings and traumatic memories have a way of surfacing in dreams and flashbacks.

On the other hand, if the trauma victim can tell friends how lonely, devastated, or ashamed he or she feels, and the friend continues to care, he or she will start to feel safe and lovable once again.

Sexual Issues

A person who has been sexually assaulted needs special care from his or her partner. Any subsequent act of lovemaking can be a reminder of the assault, so the loved one has to be very careful not to pressure the victim to have sex.

One young woman's husband was understandably enraged about her rape. However, he was more wrapped up in his own rage than he was in hers. After the rape, he forced her into having sex, claiming he wanted to erase the image of the man who raped her. Needless to say, this second "rape" compounded the original trauma.

Abstaining from sex in a married relationship requires an understanding, loving partner. This person knows how traumatic the experience has been for the victim and recognizes how traumatic sex will probably seem again. He therefore lets the victim make the decision as to when to resume this aspect of their relationship.

Honesty

Friends and relatives need to be honest when dealing with a trauma victim, especially when the victim's behavior is inappropriate. Often victims are so wrapped up in their pain that they don't recognize when their anger is irrational or directed at the wrong person.

Children especially need to know someone is concerned enough to set limits on their behavior. After a traumatic experience, they may feel out of control. If they cannot bring themselves under control, they need a loving adult to do it for them. Setting limits and pointing out unacceptable behavior are gestures of people who care.

If your uncle, a combat veteran, gets upset when bills come due and starts ranting and raving, it is OK to tell him he is scaring you. Ranting and raving around others is not appropriate behavior; he needs to hear this. The victim's goal is to heal from his trauma and reconnect with others. He will not be able to reconnect if he is scaring people off.

Abuse Issues

When Rick's stepfather married his mother and moved into their house, Rick was fourteen. He had always been an independent kid, taking care of his mother following his father's death when Rick was six. He was actually relieved he had a stepfather who could take over the job of caring for his mother. He figured his life would improve now . . . until his stepfather started coming into his bedroom at night, looking for sexual comfort.

Rick could not depend on his mother for help; after all, he had been the one to hold up his mother all those years. At first Rick tried to pretend it was not happening; then he tried to tell himself it was not too bad because his stepfather only wanted to touch him. When his stepfather forced himself on Rick one night, he knew he could not handle this situation in silence anymore. But whom could he tell? Certainly not his mother.

When he got to school that day, Rick went immediately to the counselor's office and told her what was happening at home. The counselor believed him and contacted the police. Rick was not sure what was going to happen, but he sure had not expected the police to take him to a juvenile shelter, which is what they did at the end of the school day. The police officers explained to his mother that the stepfather had been molesting Rick and that her son could not return to the home until the stepfather was gone. Rick's mother was plainly upset, torn between protecting her son and keeping her husband. After a frightening night spent in the shelter, Rick was allowed to go home with an aunt. He could not decide if he had done the right thing by telling because everyone was so upset in the family.

Although his mother agreed to divorce the stepfather so he would avoid prosecution, she welcomed him back into the house a few days at a time. After a year had passed, he was living there with Rick and his mother again. Rick moved out; he was angry that he had ended up feeling like the bad guy, as if this whole mess had been his fault. He knew his mother believed him, but he also knew his mother was not strong enough to go through life without someone to lean on. His mother preferred the husband to her son. So, even though she believed Rick, she did not value Rick enough to support him. To make matters worse, nobody thought to offer Rick counseling for the months of abuse he had endured.

A child abuse victim will recover more quickly if he or she has a support system. Ideally, the parents are that support, but what if the perpetrator is the parent? In such cases, it is vital that a loved one believe the victim's story. If the nonabusing parent does not believe the child and the perpetrator is still around, the child remains in danger. The perpetrator needs to be removed from the home to guarantee the child's safety. That does not mean the nonabusing parent must divorce the perpetrator, but he or she must see that the perpetrator receives treatment and counseling. Relying only on the perpetrator's promise to change sets the child up for further trauma.

Ironically, when the police step in, they usually remove the victim from the abusive home. This is meant to reassure the child, but more often than not it convinces the child that he or she did something wrong because the child feels as if he or she is the one being punished. The victim is the one who is isolated from the family.

Family members must strongly consider the possibility that the child is telling the truth. Sexual abuse is not something children easily talk about. They typically blame themselves for the adult's behavior, and as a result, feel ashamed and soiled. It is with tremendous reluctance that children bring these stories to their parents. If the family member immediately discounts the story and does not bother to look into it, the victim has nowhere else to go. The victim may think no one will believe him or her and that nowhere is safe.

If the perpetrator is another relative, the victim's parents must act in the child's best interests, even when that means confronting the relative. The victim first needs his parents to put a stop to the abuse. Ensuring the victim's safety means never leaving the victim alone with the relative. Usually it means getting the relative out of the house.

Many years ago our friends' five-year-old son was molested by his great-uncle. When his parents found out that the uncle had been fondling the boy at a family get-together, they were enraged. The father wanted to press charges, but the uncle's family talked him out of it. The boy's grandmother said, "We'll see that it doesn't happen again. If you press charges, then everyone will know and then think how the boy will feel. Just drop the whole thing and let it stay in the family."

The boy's parents agreed, but they didn't feel good about it. They never left the boy alone with his uncle, but their anger didn't subside: The boy had been abused, but the perpetrator was not punished.

The parents had responded supportively by believing the child and taking steps to ensure his safety. But in wanting to keep the abuse a secret, the uncle's family had not been similarly supportive. Keeping secrets makes the victim continue to feel dirty and ashamed. People who abuse children need more help than their families can give them. Helping to keep their behavior a secret allows them to continue doing what they have been doing. Loved ones do not necessarily have to press charges to ensure that the abuse will stop, but they do need to force the abuser to get treatment. Sometimes pressing charges is the only way to force the perpetrator into treatment.

A Supportive Community

A supportive community, including neighbors, police, professionals, and the media, reaffirms the victim's experiences. It says, "Yes, you are right to feel outraged. What happened to you was terrible, and your well-being matters to us."

That is why the Vietnam Memorial in Washington, D.C., is so important. When soldiers returned from the Vietnam War, there were no parades or yellow ribbons in honor of their service. More often than not, soldiers left the battlefields, boarded a commercial airliner, and arrived home alone, in civilian clothes, and without fanfare. They did not come back as troops. Many were berated for being soldiers in an unpopular war, even though they had been drafted and had not enlisted voluntarily.

Men and women who fought in the Persian Gulf War, however, returned to great acclaim, as did the soldiers who successfully fought in World Wars I and II. A grateful nation could not take away the soldiers' horrible experiences, but it could make them feel that they had endured terror for the greater good. There was no such gratitude for the returning Vietnam veterans, which made their wartime experiences that much harder to bear. Sometimes it seemed like the only people who understood their traumas were other veterans. When the Vietnam Memorial was erected many years later to honor the soldiers who had died in battle or were missing in action, Vietnam veterans at last had something that paid tribute to their service. By supporting the memorial, people were telling these veterans that Vietnam War soldiers had an important place in history, too.

When a young girl named Polly Klaus was kidnapped in California, her community banded together to search for her, to post signs in other towns, and to staff hotlines. Hollywood actress Winona Ryder put up money as a reward for information leading to Polly's safe return. And the community support did not end when Polly was found dead. After it was revealed that Polly's abductor had committed other felonies in the past, citizens lobbied statewide for stiffer penalties for repeat offenders. While the community support could not bring Polly back to her parents, it must have made the loss somewhat easier to bear. The community shared in the pain, making the parents' trauma a shared experience.

When disasters strike, whole communities rally around the victims. The Red Cross erected tent cities for the many Floridians made homeless by Hurricane Andrew while other organizations and states sent food, supplies, and volunteers. When the floods of 1993 in the American Midwest ruined crops and buried towns, supportive people were back at the post offices with more boxes of food and supplies. Expressions of goodwill and concrete support make the trauma victims feel appreciated, not scorned as nuisances.

When Timothy McVeigh bombed the Murrah Federal Building in Oklahoma City in April 1995, many cities and towns came together to offer support to the survivors and victims' families. Nowhere was that more evident than in Tulsa, the sister city just two hours up the turnpike from Oklahoma City. Tulsa sent Red Cross workers and mental health professionals down to help trauma victims, as well as manpower to comb through the building for bodies. Tulsa residents put up many signs along the turnpike expressing support for the victims, remembering their friends and relatives in Oklahoma City, and mourning their losses with them. Victims' families said they were touched and comforted by the larger community's outpouring of sympathy and compassion.

A similar sense of community was forged in the aftermath of the World Trade Center attacks. New Yorkers are not often associated with compassion, neighborliness, or concern, but within minutes of the collapse of the towers, thousands of city residents sprang into action. In addition to the rescue workers, firefighters, and police officers who poured into the area to offer their assistance (at great risk to their personal safety), makeshift volunteer centers around the city received more offers of help from regular citizens than they could possibly use. People who badly wanted to help in some concrete way were turned away, and some agencies received more donated emergency supplies than they could store and transport. So many people went to donate blood that it was not unusual to wait for eight hours to finally reach the head of the line. Neighbors who had never introduced themselves before the tragedy were suddenly asking after each other's friends and relatives and checking on each other in the succeeding days and weeks. Customers of stores in the World Trade Center area went out of their way to inquire after their favorite clerks, and hairdressers sought information on their clients who they knew worked in the towers. The sense of community and solidarity spread beyond the city limits, too, as blood donations, financial assistance, and words of comfort and support poured in from all over the country and the world. New York City is often described as an alienating place, but in the wake of the World Trade Center attacks, New Yorkers, though badly shaken, did not feel alone.

A supportive community believes that "bad things happen to good people," not that "people get what they deserve." The world is an unpredictable place, and bad things happen all the time. Although we cannot always prevent or foresee a traumatic event, we can do our best to survive it and respond supportively so other victims will survive, too. Trauma victims still have to work through their experiences by themselves, but those who have the support of their loved ones and community will survive the traumas best.

7 Positive Things You Can Do

Trying to escape the pain of a trauma does not usually work. The only positive way to deal with your experience is to confront it. Facing the pain is intended to empower you. You are not empowered when you are running away from your fears.

After a disaster such as a fire, flood, or tornado, teams of professionals usually arrive at the site to help survivors cope with the trauma. These support groups tend to be mini-marathon sessions at first, where victims can talk out their feelings with others who have gone through the same experience. The groups are helpful for two reasons: They get the victims and survivors talking instead of burying their pain, and they help victims and survivors bond with others who have also survived the disaster.

What is initially scary about a disaster is that the victim feels so alone. Support groups get the victims and survivors together and help them sort out how they feel. Groups have a greater capacity to bear pain than any one individual can alone. Survivors can scream and cry without fearing that their pain is too much for one therapist to handle. There is also an instant camaraderie between people who have been through a trauma. Sharing pain helps to lessen it.

Groups can be daunting with so much emotion clustered in one place. If you are too immersed in your own pain, you might try some individual work until you feel ready for a group experience. While groups are able to shoulder a lot of collective hurt, they also stir up a lot of pain for others who may not yet be able to tolerate it. You can learn how others managed their pain and find out some tips for navigating the mental health care system and recovery process, but if you are newly traumatized, the depth of feeling may be too much for you at this time.

Hospitals and mental health centers are quick to respond to community tragedies as well. Having crisis intervention workers report to schools in which shootings have occurred, for example, increases the number of victims and survivors reached. Many people are skeptical of outside groups offering free counseling, but when the counselors are in the schools, they are no longer considered outsiders.

Education and Self-Soothing Techniques

Not everyone who has been traumatized needs psychotherapy. Sometimes, it is enough to give the survivor time to calm down and then advise him what symptoms he might experience. For example, if a person knows that he may have nightmares for a while, he may not fear them so much.

Victims will also be angry, paranoid, and numb at times, sometimes swinging wildly between these emotions. It would be easier if the bad feelings came all at once and then went away for good, but that does not happen. If you realize that you will have good days interspersed with bad days, you will be less likely to succumb the first time a good day turns bad. It is just part of the healing process.

One useful way for you to manage your feelings would be to develop some self-soothing techniques, which are positive ways to calm yourself. You might try listening to soothing music (or for some people, listening to raucous, loud, cathartic music), drawing in coloring books with kids' big chunky crayons, rocking stuffed animals or dolls in a rocking chair, or climbing around on a jungle gym.

Whatever is helpful to you (and not hurtful to others) in reducing your emotional pain is a self-soothing technique, even if you think you are now too old to do it. Rocking is one of the best self-soothing techniques around. The back-and-forth motion is particularly soothing; it is reminiscent of the nurturing mother rocking her baby to sleep.

Many people derive comfort from keeping a journal of daily thoughts, feelings, and experiences. Any old notebook will do, or you can invest money and buy a special book just for your journal writing. You do not have to write complete sentences; you do not even have to spell words correctly. No one need ever read it but you. The whole point is to write down what you are thinking or feeling so you can reflect on it later and perhaps make some sense out of it. Some people write their thoughts and feelings down just to get rid of them for a while. If you stew a lot, playing and replaying certain memories in your head, you might try writing everything down. This may help you achieve some distance and separation from the traumatic memories, getting them out of your head and onto paper.

Another thing you could do is to play a game that requires your full concentration. Some people like crossword puzzles or board games. Some people like to vent their hostility through video games. Some people take up running, as it wears them out physically, releases endorphins (the body's natural "feel good" chemicals), and releases pent-up stress.

Finally, some people find renewed hope in attending religious services or going to concerts. They derive comfort from listening to the music or sermons in a communal setting and escaping from their obsessive, repetitive thoughts for a short period.

Handling Flashbacks

There are several positive things you can do to help you handle flashbacks. If you are prone to having them, you would be well served by planning ahead of time a strategy to deal with them. Keep a grounding object close at hand, such as a rock or a recent picture of your family or your house. That way, if you find yourself having a flashback, you will have an object ready to grasp that will reorient you to the present.

Grounding yourself, touching concrete things around you and naming them, will remind you that you are here in the present, not back there in the past again. When you start to experience a flashback, look around yourself to help keep you here in the present. Talk out loud to yourself if necessary to remind yourself where you are, what day it is, how old you are, and so on.

Hold your grounding object. Feel the strength of the rock, or look at the recent family photo and remind yourself you are not a helpless little kid anymore. Grounding objects are especially powerful if given to you by powerful people. Often therapists will give their clients what we call transitional objects. These are essentially grounding objects because they convey the strength of the therapist to the client who might need to hold the object when feeling particularly stressed.

Try to relax during a flashback, and keep breathing. When people tense up, they will breathe in a shallow way that increases the likelihood of hyperventilation. Hyperventilating just feeds your anxiety and makes it worse. Slow down your breathing, and concentrate on it. It will calm you.

In the midst of a flashback, it is important to remind yourself that you have already survived the worst. The original traumatic event is long over; you are still OK and alive. Once you return to reality from a flashback, be especially kind to yourself. If you prefer to be alone, comfort yourself. Rest and talk yourself through your fears. If you want others to comfort you, seek them out. Tell them you have had a bad dream—or a flashback, if they understand those—and ask for what you need: someone to listen to you, or someone to hold you.

Flashbacks are not a sign of a worsening condition. They are just the traumatized person's way of trying to make sense of an overwhelmingly bad experience. You can learn to manage a flashback. After all, a flashback is no more substantial than a mirage; you were strong enough to have survived the actual event.

Medication

For single-event traumas, medication is usually not recommended. Antianxiety medications, such as Valium, are not very helpful in the long run, and they can easily be abused. These pills offer a temporary respite from anxiety, but they do nothing to erase the trauma.

The reason people abuse the class of drugs known as benzodiazepines (brand names include Xanax, Ativan, and Valium) is that they mix up the secondary benefits with the primary ones. The purpose of these medications is to relax the individual and reduce his or her symptoms of anxiety. In the beginning, though, a pleasant side effect is the dreamy quality that accompanies the pill. People often confuse the pill's effectiveness with the strength of this side effect. But the body gets used to the pills after a while, and the secondary effect—that pleasant sensation—goes away. Thinking the pill is not working anymore, people take larger doses and continue increasing them each time their bodies adapt to the new dose. However, they are wrong in their assumption that the pill is not doing its job. It still manages their anxiety, but they equate its effectiveness with whether or not they are feeling that pleasant sensation. Increasing their doses over time obviously leads to drug dependence.

The other problem with benzodiazepines is the disinhibiting effect. This medication, like alcohol, makes a person more likely to do and say things he or she would not when sober. Consequently, people may be apt to say things to their loved ones without thinking, creating even more strains in their relationships. Furthermore, short-term memory loss is associated with the regular use of benzodiazepines. People will readily forget some of the hurtful things they have said over time, although people on the receiving end will not. Most important, the victim's memory of the trauma will not be forgotten no matter how many pills are taken and still needs to be addressed directly.

Better choices are beta-blocking agents, which are medications used to treat physical signs of stress such as heart palpitations, sweating, and shaky knees. If you have to confront frightening situations that remind you of a trauma suffered in the past, these medications may help desensitize you to a particular fear. You take them fifteen minutes or so before you are likely to encounter the source of your fears. With your physical symptoms of anxiety under control, you will be better able to manage your emotional symptoms.

If, for example, you were attacked by a rabid dog running loose in your neighborhood, you would no doubt be traumatized both by the dog and by the painful rabies shots you had to take. Later, you might have trouble walking past the house of the people who have two German shepherds that bark menacingly from behind their fence. If you must walk past this house to get to school, you are going to have to master your fear. The beta-blocking agents prescribed by your doctor will help get you started. They will manage your physical symptoms, so you can confront your fears. Beta blockers are not meant to be a permanent solution. They are only meant to help you get started on the path of grappling with your anxiety. After a while, you will be able to manage without medication.

Antidepressants

Antidepressants are helpful if your post-traumatic stress symptoms are complicated by grief, anxiety, or obsessive thinking. Antidepressants work by allowing more of the brain chemicals serotonin and norepinephrine to circulate in your brain. For reasons not yet known to scientists, a decline in these chemicals precipitates or exacerbates a depression. Trauma can alter brain chemistry, leaving you depleted of these mood-boosting chemicals. Antidepressants readjust the balance of your brain chemistry and, by doing so, positively affect your mood. Long-term psychotherapy may help ease depression, but medication will speed recovery.

The newer antidepressants, called selective serotonin reuptake inhibitors (SSRIs), target the symptoms of both depression and anxiety. Doctors prefer them because they have fewer side effects than the older tricyclic antidepressants, and they carry less of a risk of fatal overdose. The one exception may be Trazodone, a tricyclic antidepressant. Doctors frequently prescribe this medication in very low doses as a sleep aid. Because they prescribe it in such small doses, doctors are not relying on its antidepressant effects. Instead, they are relying on its secondary benefit—its side effect—that happens to be sedation. Trazodone makes a good choice for a sleeping pill, as it is not addictive.

A problem with the SSRIs is that they are expensive. If you do not have health insurance to cover the cost of prescriptions, you can expect to pay at least $60 a month for the lowest dose. Of the SSRIs, which include Prozac, Paxil, Zoloft, and Luvox, Zoloft is now being marketed as the treatment of choice for many people with PTSD. In addition to combating anxiety and obsessive thinking, the SSRIs are all useful in reducing the irritability that often accompanies PTSD. What seems to happen is the SSRI allows the person more time to think before he or she acts impulsively and in anger.

Bear in mind that there are no pills to get rid of anger. The person who has experienced a trauma has to come to terms with the resulting rage and sense of injustice. You succeed in doing this only when you examine your feelings and work your way through the grief process. Sometimes doctors prescribe "atypical antipsychotics" to treat signs of extreme agitation in people with PTSD. These newer antipsychotic medications (Seroquel, Zyprexa, and Risperdal) have fewer side effects than the older antipsychotics, such as Thorazine, Stelazine, Mellaril, and Haldol. They work by helping the individual think more clearly and less obsessively. However, they are not intended to be used permanently.

Other medications your doctor might prescribe include lithium and buspirone. In small doses, lithium is useful in managing anger. Though often prescribed for bipolar disorders such as manic depression, you do not have to be bipolar to benefit from lithium. So if your doctor prescribes this, it does not mean he or she thinks you are also a manic-depressive. Buspirone is a nonaddicting medication that seems to help with intrusive thoughts and nightmares.

Summary

Educate your family and friends about your symptoms and treatment. The more they understand your situation, the more supportive they can be. Do not make a secret of your trauma. You don't have to take out ads in the newspaper, but you should not behave as if you have done something dirty or shameful. Bad things happen; that is a fact of life.

Let your family and friends know what you need. If you feel like talking, find someone who will listen. Talking is a release that will lighten your load of anxiety. It also allows your friends and family to help others to see that PTSD is a very real condition. If you have been assaulted on the way to your car, you are going to have a lot of anxiety about walking to your car after dark in the future. Do not try to make light of your feelings. Your terror is understandable and very real. Most people in your situation would feel the same adrenaline surge when alone on a dark street at night.

PTSD is not overcome by thinking of other things. Survivors of trauma have to work hard to confront and overcome fears. Do not pretend that it is no big deal. It is hard work, and you have a right to be proud of yourself for taking the steps to heal. Nonetheless, you can let go of the scary feelings when you need a break. The fact that you are not trying to bury your feelings does not mean you have to think about them all the time. It is OK to put them aside every so often, as long as you are consciously putting them aside. Suppressing is different from repressing or pretending the memories are not there. When you suppress, you know the memories are still there until you are ready to confront them again. Above all, be kind to yourself. Eat well, get plenty of sleep (or rest, if sleep is hard to come by), and spend time with people who can offer comfort to you.

Choosing the Right Therapist

Some practical matters help decide which therapist is right for you. Therapists, whether social workers, psychologists, or psychiatrists, charge from $85 an hour and up, so most people need to rely on their health insurance to pay the bill.

When you use your insurance coverage, you have to go along with what the professional insurance company says it will cover. Most places have their own clinicians on staff or several in the community to whom they refer. Today, the emphasis is on short-term psychotherapy, usually crisis resolution. Your insurance company will probably pay 50 percent of the cost of your treatment if you see someone it recommends and you do not exceed the number of sessions that the plan covers. Some policies cover 100 percent of the time-limited sessions.

If you do not have insurance, or do not choose to use it, then you pay either the full cost of treatment or a sliding scale fee based upon your income. If you cannot find someone you can afford, check out the mental health centers in your community. You can find these places in the yellow pages of your phone book under "mental health." They offer a variety of low-cost services, but there is often a waiting list.

Another problem is that when you rely on insurance coverage, your insurer has the right to obtain information on your diagnosis and treatment goals. If you or your parents can afford it, you might prefer paying for therapy out-of-pocket for privacy reasons. While private therapists can be expensive, there are some alternatives. Community mental health centers or private organizations often offer therapy at a fee that you can afford. School guidance counselors can help you explore these more affordable options.

Credentials

It does not really matter what type of professional you choose. A clinical social worker has received his or her master's degree or Ph.D. in social work and then specialized in clinical (counseling) work. If he or she is licensed, a clinical social worker will have passed a rigorous national exam and worked for at least two years under the supervision of another licensed clinical social worker. Many social workers specialize and provide much of the counseling at mental health agencies.

A clinical psychologist has probably received a Ph.D. in clinical psychology and passed a rigorous national exam to become licensed. He or she specializes in counseling. Other psychologists specialize in research or school counseling. An advantage to psychologists is that they can administer tests if necessary and interpret the results, although you do not need psychological testing to determine whether or not you are suffering from PTSD.

A psychiatrist is a medical doctor who specializes in psychiatry, usually spending the bulk of training in psychiatric hospitals. Unlike clinical social workers and psychologists, a psychiatrist can prescribe medication. Being an M.D., a psychiatrist's services are the most expensive.

Even if you think you need medication to help cope with your symptoms, you do not need to see a psychiatrist first. Any social worker or psychologist will consult with a doctor if necessary and refer you for possible medication.

Whether you see a social worker, psychologist, or psychiatrist, what counts is your ability to work with that person. The vast majority of therapists are very good at what they do, which is making you feel safe, understood, and empowered. They have worked long and hard to gain their training and licensing. Having earned a license—not an easy process—a therapist is accountable to the licensing organization. This means that you will have greater legal recourse if the therapist does something unethical. You cannot sue a therapist for not making you well, however.

There is one exception to the rule about licensure. If you are seeing a therapist at a community mental health center, you may be assigned a therapist who is not currently licensed. It takes a therapist two years of supervision by a licensed professional to apply for licensure. There has to be a setting where license-eligible therapists can practice and receive supervision, and mental health centers are frequently the places of choice, as they tend to be teaching institutions for therapists and doctors alike. You can be sure your unlicensed therapist is receiving ample supervision and consultation there, and you can always appeal to his or her supervisor if you have any concerns.

Personality and Gender

Everyone has issues to work out, whether the therapist is male or female. If you've been raped, you may think you need to see a woman, but often seeing a man is helpful in showing you how to trust men again. Clients usually find that different issues crop up no matter who they are seeing, and all are important to resolve.

Personality is an issue. Sometimes a client just does not like working with a certain therapist. As long as you are not running away from therapy altogether (switching therapists every two weeks because you do not like them is a form of running away), you may need a change. Some therapists simply clash with your personality. You are going to be unburdening yourself to this person, and you will not feel comfortable doing that if you find the therapist abrasive or arrogant. Some therapists are more direct than others; they ask many questions and make interpretations. Others sit back and let you struggle with topics without offering much prompting or assistance. Neither way is necessarily better. Some people do not like it if the therapist does more talking than they do. Others think they are not getting their money's worth unless the therapist does all the talking.

It is OK to interview several therapists before you commit yourself to treatment. You should be able to get an idea of how warm they are, how direct, and how busy. You can ask the therapists how they might treat you for PTSD, but that is a hard question to answer without actually getting to know the client and his or her specific trauma. A better question to ask might be what their experience has been in treating people with PTSD.

You will want someone who is familiar with trauma, its symptoms, and effective treatments. What you need first and foremost is someone who knows what you are going through and how you can best recover.

The Therapeutic Experience

Therapy is designed to take you through the three steps of recovery: finding security, mourning, and reconnecting. The first goal is to make you safe. Toward that end, the therapist may suggest medication—particularly if you are suicidal or feel severely agitated. Medication will reduce the symptoms of hyperarousal and depression.

The therapist may suggest a plan of action to secure your safety at home: a few days at a battered women's shelter if you are in an abusive situation at home, or having a friend stay with you for a while if you live alone. Sometimes the therapist may show you relaxation techniques to help you manage your anxiety.

Contrary to what you might think, you will not unburden yourself to the therapist in the first few sessions. You will only give enough information to clarify your safety concerns once a diagnosis has been made. Relating your traumatic memories comes a little later. Your therapist will first want to ensure your safety and relative stability. Often a client is in a hurry and starts reliving memories before he or she is able to tolerate the pain they generate. Your therapist will want you to go slowly.

Remembrance and mourning comprise the second stage of recovery. Unfortunately, you cannot get better without looking back at your pain, reexperiencing it, and then mourning. When you start talking about your memories, you will find your intrusive symptoms increasing. The more you think about things and tell your therapist, the more memories will surface. Sometimes the memories come first; sometimes only the feelings come. In either event, you will probably start to feel scared, sad, or angry. A good therapist monitors your intrusive symptoms and slows down the process of delving into your past when you are becoming too stressed. One thing you should remember, however, is that no matter how gradually you recover your memories, you will not be functioning your best during this time. Most of your energy will be going toward maintaining your stability during this painful but necessary process; be kind to yourself.

Although your job in therapy is to uncover the memories, sometimes it is also to put them aside until you are strong enough to face them all. This is called suppression, and it is a conscious act. You are not denying the feelings; instead, you are knowingly setting them aside for the moment. As long as you eventually come back to them, you are not doing anything wrong.

The ultimate goal of therapy, though, cannot be to remember everything in accurate detail because that is not going to be possible. Memory is susceptible to influence. The goal is to gain perspective on all that you can remember so that you can reframe your thinking of the world as a dangerous, threatening place.

The process of remembering and mourning will be the hardest part of recovery. Some clients try to get around the pain by recalling the memories but not the feelings that went with them. That's called intellectualization, and it is a defense mechanism designed to reduce anxiety. It means you remain in your head, analyzing and diagnosing without "feeling the feelings" you are talking about. You can't get better by keeping feelings and experiences separate. To integrate your experiences, you have to reexperience the feelings. Think not only of what happened to you, but how you felt and what you heard, thought, saw, and smelled at the time. Anyone can name a feeling; experiencing it is another story. Remembering traumatic experiences sets you up to mourn, which you must do to get rid of the trauma's hold on you.

Oddly enough, recapturing the memories and sharing them helps to put them into perspective. By telling your story out loud, you do not "lose the story," but you trade the shame and humiliation for dignity.

A major problem for abuse survivors (who were told as children to keep what was happening a secret) is to later confide in a therapist. It may feel as if you're breaking a family rule; you're telling the secret. Expect to feel guilty, as that is normal because you have probably carried your secret so long. But remind yourself that you were too young to make such an agreement, and you are not being disloyal in telling your story now. Perpetrators count on the loyalty—or fear—of their victims to keep them from being apprehended and stopped. As you reveal your secrets, you will be better able to make sense of what happened to you. The secret is not your shame; the shame belongs to the perpetrator.

Mourning

No matter what your trauma may have been, you have lost something important. You might have lost all your possessions in a fire, your loved ones in an accident, or your belief in a safe, predictable world. People who survived Hurricane Andrew in 1992 lost most of what they owned. Roofs were torn off of houses, and their contents were blown miles away. Some people were not insured, and they lost everything they owned and everything they had worked on for years. Those who lived were grateful for their lives, but they had lost a lot, including their peace of mind.

Mourning is the hardest part of therapy. It hurts. Some people prefer feeling angry to feeling sad. Anger is often empowering; it makes you feel strong. Grief can make you feel weak and passive. Unfortunately, you cannot let go of something until you have mourned it. Some victims and survivors refuse to mourn out of pride. They think they are standing up to their abuser by denying their pain. In effect, they are saying, "See? You didn't hurt me." But the perpetrator does win if you cannot be a whole person again. Reexperiencing all of your emotions is an act of courage and resistance. Survivors of the Nazi Holocaust showed us just how horrendous their experiences had been by unearthing all their pain. Had they not mourned, we would not have understood the depth of their anguish and suffering.

Some people avoid mourning by concentrating on seeking revenge. Nothing anyone does can ever compensate for a harm already done; that harm cannot be undone. You cannot get back a loved one who has died, you cannot get back your virginity, and you cannot get back peace of mind. Victims and survivors often fantasize about revenge, believing that any victory over the perpetrator will erase the humiliation of their trauma.

One of my clients had been abused as a child by her father. At one point in therapy, she wrote a letter to her father's employer, describing her years of abuse at the hands of her father. Clearly, she would have gotten nothing out of exposing her father. In fact, it probably would have added to her embarrassment and powerlessness. What she really wanted was for her father to admit he had hurt her and say that he wanted to make up for it.

Although she primarily wanted to hurt him, she also wanted him to validate her assumptions. She remembered being sexually abused at night, but it was a long time ago, and he never had acted during the day as if he had done anything wrong. She wanted to hear from him that he had actually abused her. Since he denied it when she confronted him recently, she was furious at being rendered powerless a second time. "I can't make him admit what he did, but I can hurt him otherwise. I'll make him pay," she thought.

Nursing your sense of injustice and waiting for your abuser to admit his wrongdoing are ways to hang onto the pain. Likewise, immediately forgiving your abuser or the person who killed your loved one is actually a way to avoid mourning. Some people tell themselves, "I've forgiven you," and think that is the end of it. It doesn't work that way. You do not need to forgive your perpetrator as much as you need to forgive yourself. Do not confuse embracing life again with embracing your abuser; they are not the same. Letting go of the hate that binds you to your enemy does not mean you now like this person. You and your therapist can work out your feelings once you have brought them out into the open.

Reconnecting with others is the final stage in recovery. You have mourned your losses, and now you need to get on with your life. Humans were not meant to live isolated lives. People can handle so much more pain when there are others to share it. Some people have been so traumatized by their experiences that they do not know how to socialize anymore. Support groups are helpful at this point because they offer a way to get back into the community.

If you were abused as a child, this is the stage of therapy at which to challenge family secrets. My client would have felt better about herself if she had waited until after mourning her losses before trying to wrangle a confession from her father. At this point, as long as you are prepared for any possible outcome, you are ready to come forth with your secrets. The goal is to stop carrying the secret, not to convince the abuser of his or her wrongdoing. You have known all along that the abuse was wrong; you do not need him or her to agree with you. While an apology might be nice, it does not erase the trauma.

But you do not have to be a party to family secrets anymore. Once you get things out in the open, you lose your shame and humiliation. After all, what happened to you was not your fault.

Your work is essentially done in therapy when you realize you can be happy again and you are now engaged in healthy relationships. Your physiological symptoms of trauma will be under control, and you will be better able to tolerate your memories and the feelings associated with them.

For people with dissociative identity disorder, the therapist's job is much more complicated. In addition to helping the client mourn his losses, the therapist has to help him integrate the different alters into one functioning person.

Sometimes, that is not always possible, and the best the therapist can do is get the different parts functioning together as a unit.

Problems in Therapy

Therapy is not a smooth process in which the client makes steady progress in an uphill fashion. More often that not, you take one step forward and two steps back before you begin to move forward steadily. Resistance is a term therapists use to describe a client's reluctance to work on issues. Most clients, and many therapists, do not recognize the resistance at first. Some clients skip appointments, offering plausible reasons for their absences. Sometimes clients do not bring up important issues until they are winding up a session and know full well they do not have time to pursue that issue. Clients resist the most when they want to avoid their pain.

Transference is another issue that sometimes hinders and sometimes helps along the therapeutic process. Transference is when you have feelings for your therapist similar to those you have for other authority figures. For example, one PTSD sufferer wore short skirts and tight sweaters to her therapy appointments. Having always related to men sexually in the past, she started doing the same with her therapist. Most of the time, transference issues cloud the therapeutic relationship. Clients tend to love their therapists, whom they see as rescuers, and hate them at the same time because inevitably therapists fail to live up to their clients' expectations. If a client doesn't resolve his transference from one authority figure (usually a parent) to another (the therapist), he will simply get out of therapy when the situation gets sticky.

The opposite thing happens when therapists have feelings for their clients that really reflect how they feel toward others in their lives. This is called countertransference. Sometimes therapists identify so strongly with your experiences that they attempt to do too much for you. They allow you to call them too often between sessions, or they make important decisions for you in session. This unlimited phone contact may tell you that your therapist really cares about you, but orchestrating every move you make in your life actually works against you. The purpose of therapy is to empower you. If your therapist responds to your phone calls all the time, she allows you to rely on her instead of on yourself. If your therapist thinks of you too much as a victim, she will be more likely to handle problems for you that you should actually handle yourself.

Countertransference is something the therapist has to deal with herself; consulting with other professionals about her cases helps her work on any countertransference issues she might have. You just need to realize that a therapist who does not try to rescue you every time you think you have a problem is really doing you a favor. The greatest gift a therapist can give you is the knowledge that you can rescue yourself.

Your therapist serves you by listening to whatever it is you have to discuss. Sometimes, particularly with young children, the therapist just plays games with her clients or watches them play with toys in her office. Traumatized children reenact their traumas, and the therapist can make observations and interpretations by watching or engaging in the play. Sometimes, trauma victims cannot find words for their feelings. Their therapist might suggest they draw a picture of how they are feeling. Art therapy is very helpful for some people who cannot put their feelings into words.

A trauma is never fully resolved, no matter how much time passes. Different stressors may propel a person back into therapy. Someone who was abused as a child might resolve the trauma through therapy but feel nervous all over again when her daughter approaches the age at which she herself was abused. Some people manage to keep their traumas under wraps until their perpetrator dies. Then, all the memories return in force. Some people who have survived terrible natural disasters deal with their feelings by moving. If their children decide to move back to the area of the disaster, these traumatized individuals often feel a resurgence of their old symptoms.

Therapy is an open-ended situation. You go through the steps of recovery, and you feel better. You do not have to stay in therapy all your life. If the symptoms return, you simply go back for some additional work, which does not mean going through the whole process all over again or for the same length of time. It is usually easier the second time around.

The goal of therapy is to help you find your integrity. For most people, the long, hard work is well worth it.

Need for Hospitalization

Most people do not need to be hospitalized for the treatment of PTSD, but sometimes a person needs a more secure environment than what he or she has at home. Sometimes in the midst of therapy, a person becomes overwhelmed by all the memories and feelings and ceases to function. That is when others will consider hospitalizing him or her.

Any time a person is thinking of suicide, particularly if he or she has a plan and the means by which to carry it out, he or she should be hospitalized. It is impossible to keep another person safe when the person is in an unstructured environment and free to do as he or she wants.

If a person is hallucinating or hearing voices that tell him to hurt others or himself, the person is out of touch with reality and needs hospitalization. If a person is unable to control his feelings and so is likely to harm someone else, he also needs a safe, controlled, supervised environment. In addition, society needs to be protected from potentially violent PTSD sufferers as much as they need to be protected from themselves.

Finally, if a person is unable to function and unable to take care of himself or herself, someone needs to provide that care at home or in a hospital. Hospitalization is a safety issue. If a person is not eating because he or she is too depressed to crawl out of bed, then that person is in danger of starving to death. Hospitalization provides a structured and safe environment.

9 Getting On with Your Life

Whether or not you have used therapy to help you heal from PTSD, at some point you are going to be ready to get on with your life. The first thing you need to do is trade in your victim status. If you continue to see yourself as a victim, then you have not gotten over your ordeal. You are no longer just a victim; you are now a survivor. You are still alive; you are still here. But remember—and this may sound like contradictory advice—you don't want to think of yourself as a survivor forever either. And why not? After all, isn't surviving a trauma a good thing?

Of course, seeing yourself as a survivor is better than seeing yourself as a victim. A victim has things done to him or her; a survivor rises above those things. Survivors are strong, and you have been strong enough to put your trauma into perspective. The problem is continually thinking in terms of the trauma. When you call yourself a survivor, you are still defining yourself in terms of what happened to you. At some point, you have got to get back to being just a person—neither a victim nor a survivor. Having survived an ordeal should not be the first thing others know about you. You are a person first.

A friend of mine who experienced a bitter divorce used to tell everyone she met that she had survived a marriage made in hell and a divorce that was worse. People got tired of hearing about her experiences. After a couple of years and several months of therapy, she stopped dragging the divorce and her survivor status into every conversation. At the same time, she started to live again. When she was no longer defining herself in terms of the failed marriage, she was no longer tied to an ex-husband who had dominated her life. By dropping the victim and survivor images, she effectively dropped him from her life. She was ready to move on.

Taking Control

When something awful has happened to you, it is easy to feel out of control. That is why it is important to regain control of your life as soon as you are able. First, take steps to recover—making yourself safe, remembering and mourning your losses, and putting them into perspective—and then set positive goals to get on with your life.

Getting away from a disaster does not mean you are running away from your trauma. A change of scenery can be healthy: Have a weekend getaway or go on a vacation. Sometimes, it is the smartest thing you can do. Learn to make decisions by yourself and not to rely too much on others to tell you what you need to do each time. Start out with small decisions, like what you want to eat this week or what clothes you feel like wearing.

As you tackle these smaller decisions, you will be more ready for the bigger ones to come. Making positive changes in your life means you are willing to take a chance on the future.

If you seek legal restitution for your trauma, be sure you can live with any outcome. Just because you know that you deserve restitution does not mean the courts will see it that way. Life is not fair, and sometimes you do not end up getting the restitution you deserve. But seeking amends can be a positive step; it indicates you are worth seeking justice for. You may also consider joining a social action group and work toward changes in the law.

If you have been raped, it is not enough to heal. Learn to protect yourself. A gun is not a solution; more gun owners than criminals get hurt by guns. Instead, learn martial arts such as tae kwon do or karate; in addition to learning to protect yourself, you will gain a feeling of strength. Even if you do not want to learn a form of martial arts, you can take a self-defense course or a rape prevention class. A strong person is one who does not simply rely on others to protect her; she takes steps to protect herself.

If you were sexually abused as a child, protect yourself and learn how to feel secure, particularly at bedtime. If that means you want to sleep with the bedroom door locked, then buy a lock and lock the door. If the noise of a fan drowns out street noises and helps lull you to sleep, you should purchase a relatively inexpensive floor fan.

Don't drink alcohol before you go to sleep, even if you think it helps make you sleepy. In the long run, alcohol is disruptive to sleep. You may fall asleep without problems, but you will awaken frequently. Limit caffeine during the day, as that will contribute to wakefulness. Do not exercise too close to bedtime, as that will also arouse your system, and you will not be able to fall asleep for a long time.

But most of all, do not obsess over how much sleep you get. You will survive even if you stay awake all night. If you have consulted a doctor and followed his or her advice, and you still have trouble sleeping on occasion, try not to worry about it. Worrying will only arouse you further.

Handling Natural Disasters

If you have survived an earthquake, a hurricane, or a tornado, you might think there is nothing you can do to protect yourself in the future. Natural disasters are not predictable. But even if nature is not totally predictable, we still have things we can do to ensure our safety. Meteorologists can forecast tornadoes and hurricanes. If you know the conditions are in place for one to develop, or one is already on its way, take steps to protect yourself and your home. Know the safest places to hide during a windstorm (either the center of your house away from windows, or the northeast corner). If you are directly in a hurricane's path, board up your windows. Then leave your house and move further inland.

If you are traveling and the sky looks threatening, keep your radio tuned to a local station. That way, you will be warned in advance if a tornado has been sighted in the area. Know to get out of your car in a windstorm and lie low in a ditch or hide under a bridge underpass.

Of course, you cannot predict an earthquake. If you live in an earthquake-prone area, make sure you know the signs of an earthquake and where to seek shelter. Prepare an escape plan should an earthquake happen in the middle of the night. Keep your house equipped with flashlights and fresh batteries and stocked with extra food and water.

Other Disasters

Learn how to drive defensively. Assume no one else knows how to drive, and be prepared for someone to do something stupid. If you give up driving after an accident, you are still just as liable to be involved in an accident as a passenger. If you have survived a fire, make sure you know what caused the fire. If the wiring was faulty in your house, have it checked by a professional. Keep smoke detectors on every floor, and periodically check that the batteries are working. Never smoke a cigarette when you are sleepy. It is too easy to fall asleep with a lit cigarette.

Realize you cannot totally control your environment. Bad things do happen to good people, and bad things can always happen again despite your best attempts to guard against them. In the case of terrorism, you cannot predict other people's behavior; all you can do is remain alert to danger, trust your instincts and strengths, and be prepared to react quickly to whatever comes your way. Most important, you must live with joy, energy, and enthusiasm. Do not let the fear of unknown and unexpected situations constrict your life and limit your experiences.

Doing Something Positive with Your Anger

Use your anger positively. It takes a lot of energy to keep memories repressed, and it takes a lot of energy to stay angry. Put that anger to other uses. Get involved in changing the laws or helping others survive similar traumas.

Start a support group. If you attend college, pursue a degree in one of the helping professions. People who have survived traumas and have taken the time to heal are excellent helpers. Take some time to explore your interests.

For women who were abused, certain medical procedures can trigger PTSD reactions. Any kind of physical exam, but particularly the annual gynecological exam, will be evocative of your past abuse. You cannot just quit having physical exams, but you can take steps to make the exams more tolerable. First of all, explain to your doctor or nurse that you were sexually or physically abused in the past. If you are uncomfortable with males, ask to be referred to a female doctor. If it is not possible to switch to a female doctor, ask for a female nurse to be present at all times.

Ask the doctor to explain every part of the procedure to you as he or she goes along. If you start feeling anxious, tell the doctor. If you are very anxious, ask to take a break. You have a right to make these requests, and most doctors will be very understanding. If you are relaxed, he or she can do a better job. If your doctor feels inconvenienced by your concerns, then he or she is not the right doctor for you. Get a different one.

Finally, employ relaxation techniques to help you manage anxiety. Take a comforting object with you and hold it throughout the exam. Focus on your breathing, slow and deep from the belly. Hold the nurse's hand if possible, or bring a trusted friend with you for the exam. Talk about ordinary things: the weather, your plans for the day, a funny story. If you cannot talk or do not feel like listening to someone else talk, bring a CD player with you and listen to some music. Gradually, you will become accustomed to these medical procedures and will realize they do not represent more abuse but instead are important procedures for maintaining your physical health.

Taking care of yourself also means knowing your own limitations. When you are too immersed in your own pain, you are not in a position to help other people with their problems. You are not mentally strong enough to take on their burdens as well as your own. That does not mean you have to push them away; rather, you should refer them to a professional. Taking care of yourself sometimes requires putting your mental health ahead of the problems of others. There is someone else around who can help them; it does not always have to be you.

Getting Better

Someone once said, "Time heals all wounds." You might think that person has never suffered a loss. But time does make the pain more bearable, as long as the grief is not buried. And after a time—usually a long time—the pain lessens. Another person once said, "Living well is the best revenge." If you can survive and hold your head up, you will have preserved your self-esteem. Your trauma did not take that from you. And that is the definition of living well—maintaining your dignity and self-worth.

Epilogue:

When Someone You Know Has Suffered a Trauma or Is Diagnosed with PTSD

1. Learn all you can about PTSD. Visit Web sites and read books and articles about your loved one's particular trauma. See the Where to Go for Help and For Further Reading sections in this book for information.

2. Let your loved one, friend, or relative talk. Do not discourage him or her from talking about the trauma. It is a release to talk even if the person ends up saying the same stuff he or she told you yesterday. Your loved one may wind up crying, but you are not the cause of this. Mourning losses is a painful process; victims need to feel the loss before they can let go of it. However, do not tell the person to cry if he or she isn't. Let him or her cry as she wishes. You will probably hear a lot about the trauma. That is because the trauma does not go away with just one telling. You are doing your friend a tremendous favor by listening. Do not underestimate your kindness, and remember that mourning losses is a very long process. Try not to set a time limit on it.

3. Do not listen if you cannot give the victim all your attention. Here are other things to avoid:

    - Cutting the victim off before he or she finishes what he or she is saying.

    - Comparing similar events in your life; pain and trauma are not comparative.

    - Do not play psychologist; refer the victim to a real psychologist or therapist.

    - Do not judge or belittle; the victim only needs you to listen and does not need to hear what you think he or she did wrong.

4. Expect your friend to have good days and bad days, but do not tolerate inappropriate behavior. If your friend is using the trauma as an excuse to be rude and mean, point it out and demand better. You are doing the victim a favor by pointing out unacceptable behavior such as swearing too much, ranting and raving at store clerks, or hiding out in the bedroom.

5. Seek to understand how your friend feels about the trauma and the future. If he or she can share feelings with you, he or she is acknowledging them to himself or herself.

6. Understand the importance of victims' support groups. These group members have been through the same or similar traumas. Understand the importance of community support and recognition.

7. Set limits on what you can do to help your friend. Even therapists have to set limits. People who have been chronically abused often tend to exhaust others with their dependence and resentment. Refer him or her to a therapist, or contact a therapist yourself, when you are in over your head.

8. If the victim sounds suicidal, report it to a therapist, teacher, minister, parent, or other appropriate adult. If you cannot locate the appropriate adult, call the police. Your friend needs help at once.

9. Do not expect your friend to get better within any set time. People heal differently. Do not put pressure on the victim to conform to your expectations. If things are dragging on with no signs of improvement, suggest that he or she see a professional. Then let the professional and your friend handle the progress.

10. Encourage your friend to think positively about his or her future. Suggest activities to involve your friend in. If your friend is trying to desensitize himself or herself to something, go along while he or she practices. If your female friend is afraid to have a gynecological exam, volunteer to go with her, keep her company, and offer her your moral support. Let your friend know that you believe things will get better. And if all else fails, help him or her plan that future. Just remember, as a friend and loved one, you do not have to do it all. You just need to be there.

Glossary

alters Separate and unique systems of personality; two or more develop in an individual with dissociative identity disorder.

antidepressant Medication used to treat PTSD when it is complicated by depression.

beta-blocking agents Medications used to treat PTSD victims. They control a person's physical reactions when facing similar stress repeatedly.

competence Being good at something.

constriction Leading a restricted life to avoid dealing with further trauma or reexperiencing pain.

countertransference The complex feelings a therapist has toward his or her client in therapy.

deficiency needs According to Abraham Maslow, a person's basic needs for survival, security, attachment, and self-esteem.

delusion A belief that is contrary to reality but that is still held firmly.

dissociative identity disorder Disorder in which an individual splits into two or more distinct personalities, called alters, who help the host personality cope with trauma.

dissociative state Trancelike state to which trauma victims resort to keep from being aware of their current trauma.

flashbacks Memories that draw the victim back into the scene of the original trauma, as if he or she were experiencing it all over again.

growth needs According to Abraham Maslow, a person's need to learn, appreciate beauty, live up to his or her potential, and lead a spiritual life.

hallucinations Things that are seen or heard that are not really there.

hyperarousal Being vigilant and always on the alert for danger.

initiative The ability to start things on one's own.

insomnia The inability to fall asleep or stay asleep.

intrusion Having the memory of a trauma continue to reinsert itself into one's consciousness either through nightmares, flashbacks, or daydreams.

paranoia Symptoms of delusions and loss of contact with reality.

perpetrator Person who commits a crime or an abuse against someone.

psychophysiologic signs Physical ailments, such as stomachaches, that mimic the victim's reaction to the initial trauma and continue to occur in times of stress.

reenactment The reliving of the original trauma through one's behavior.

regression The unconscious act of reverting to an earlier time in one's life that seemed safe and then behaving as if one were that age.

rehearsing Thinking or talking about a memory.

repetitive dreams Dreams similar in themes or exactly alike in details that one has after a trauma.

repression The unconscious act of forgetting a painful memory.

resistance A victim's reluctance to deal with issues in therapy.

rigidity Behaving in a set fashion, usually to avoid situations reminiscent of a trauma. Also, a deadening of the emotions and a loss of playfulness.

suppression The conscious act of not thinking about something painful.

transference A client's feelings for his or her therapist that often reflect feelings toward other authority figures in his or her life.

trauma Frightening event out of one's usual human experience. It may be a life-threatening event or the experience of witnessing death or injury.

Where to Go for Help

Hotlines

American Red Cross
Compassion and Information Hotline
(866) GET-INFO (438-4636)
Web site: http://www.redcross.org/index.html

National Child Abuse Hotline
Childhelp USA
(800) 4-A-CHILD (422-4453)

National Coalition Against Domestic Violence
(800) 799-7233

National Sexual Assault Hotline
(800) 656-HOPE (4673)

Town National Crisis Line
(800) 448-3000
(800) 448-1833 (TDD for hearing impaired)

Youth Crisis Hotline
(800) 448-4663

Information/Referrals

American Academy of Child and Adolescent Psychiatry
3615 Wisconsin Avenue NW
Washington, DC 20016-3007
(202) 966-7300
Web site: http://www.aacap.org/index.htm

The American Academy of Experts in Traumatic Stress
368 Veterans Memorial Highway
Commack, NY 11725
(631) 543-2217
Web site: http://www.aaets.org

American Psychiatric Association
1400 K Street NW
Washington, DC 20005
(888) 357-7924
Web site: http://www.psych.org/index.cfm

American Psychological Association
750 First Street NE
Washington, DC 20002-4242
(800) 374-2721
Web site: http://helping.apa.org/index.html

Center for Medical Help Services (CMHS)
Emergency Services and Disaster Relief Branch
5600 Fishers Lane, Room 16C-26
Rockville, MD 20857
(301) 443-4735
Web site: http://www.samhsa.gov/cmhs/cmhs.htm

International Society for Traumatic Stress Studies (ISTSS)
60 Revere Drive, Suite 500
Northbrook, IL 60062
(847) 480-9028
Web site: http://www.istss.org

National Center for PTSD
215 North Main Street
White River Junction, VT 05009
(802) 296-5132
Web site: http://www.ncptsd.org

National Center for Victims of Crime
2000 M Street NW, Suite 480
Washington, DC 20036
(800) 394-2255
Web site: http://www.ncvc.org

National Institute of Mental Health (NIMH)
NIMH Public Inquiries
6001 Executive Boulevard
Room 8184, MSC 9663
Bethesda, MD 20892-9663
(301) 443-4513
Web site: http://www.nimh.nih.gov

National Organization for Victim Assistance (NOVA)
1730 Park Road NW
Washington, DC 20010
(202) 232-6682
Web site: http://www.try-nova.org

The Rape, Abuse, and Incest Network (RAINN)
635-B Pennsylvania Avenue SE
Washington, DC 20003
(800) 656-HOPE (4673)
Web site: http://www.rainn.org

Sidran Traumatic Stress Foundation
200 East Joppa Road, Suite 207
Towson, MD 21286
(410) 825-8888
Web site: http://www.sidran.org

Treatment Programs

The Colin A. Ross Institute for Psychological Trauma
1701 Gateway, Suite 349
Richardson, TX 75080
(972) 918-9588

Post-Traumatic and Dissociative Disorders Program
The Psychiatric Institute of Washington
4228 Wisconsin Avenue NW
Washington, DC 20016
(800) 369-2273

In Canada

Anxiety Disorders Association of Ontario
797 Somerset Street West, Suite 14
Ottawa, ON K1R 6R3
(613) 729-6761
Web site: http://www.anxietyontario.com

Canadian Mental Health Association (CMHA)
2160 Yonge Street, 3rd Floor
Toronto, ON M4S 2Z3
(416) 484-7750
Web site: http://www.cmha.ca/english/index.html

Canadian Network for Mood and Anxiety Treatments
Web site: http://www.canmat.org/canmat/index.html

Canadian Traumatic Stress Network
Web site: http://www.ctsn-rcst.ca

Health Canada
A.L. 0900C2
Ottawa, ON K1A 0K9
(613) 957-2991
Web site: http://www.hc-sc.gc.ca/english/index.htm

Ontario Coalition Rape Crisis Center
(705) 268-8381

The Ottawa Anxiety and Trauma Clinic
Billings Bridge Plaza
2277 Riverside Drive, Suite 202
Ottawa, ON K1H 7X6
(613) 737-1194
Web site: http://www.anxietyandtraumaclinic.com

Ottawa Rape Crisis Centre
(613) 562-2333

Ottawa Recovered Memory Page
Web site: http://www.carleton.ca/~whovdest/ormp.html

Veterans Affairs Canada
Ste. Anne's Hospital
305, boulevard des Anciens-Combattants
Sainte-Anne-de-Bellvue, PQ H9X 1Y9
(800) 361-9287
Web site: http://www.vac-acc.gc.ca/general

Web Sites

Internet Mental Health
http://www.mentalhealth.com

MayoClinic.com
http://www.mayoclinic.com/findinformation/diseasesandconditions/invoke.cfm?id=ds00246

1-800-THERAPIST
http://www.1-800-therapist.com

PTSD Alliance
http://www.ptsdalliance.org/home3.html
(877) 507-PTSD (7873)

PTSD.com
http://www.ptsd.com

For Further Reading

Brenneis, C. Brooks. *Recorded Memories of Trauma: Transferring the Present to the Past.* Madison, CT: International Universities Press, 1999.

Coffey, Rebecca. *Unspeakable Truths and Happy Endings: Human Cruelty and the New Trauma Therapy.* Towson, MD: Sidran Press, 1998.

Foa, Edna B., Terence M. Keane, and Matthew J. Friedman, eds. *Effective Treatments for PTSD.* New York: Guilford Press, 2000.

Foa, Edna B., and Barbara Rothbaum, Ph.D. *Treating the Trauma of Rape.* New York: Guilford Press, 1998.

Herman, Judith Lewis, M.D. *Trauma and Recovery.* New York: Basic Books, 1997.

Hybels-Steer, Mariann. *Aftermath.* New York: Fireside/Simon and Schuster, Inc., 1995.

Lee, Richard S., and Mary Price Lee. *Everything You Need to Know About Natural Disasters and Post-Traumatic Stress Disorder.* New York: The Rosen Publishing Group, Inc., 1995.

Matsakis, Aphrodite. *I Can't Get Over It: A Handbook for Trauma Survivors.* New York: New Harbinger Publications, 1996.

Matsakis, Aphrodite. *Trust After Trauma: A Guide to Relationships for Survivors and Those Who Love Them.* New York: New Harbinger Publications, 1998.

Munson, Lulie, and Karen Riskin. *In Their Own Words: A Sexual Abuse Workbook for Teenage Girls.* Washington, DC: Child Welfare League of America, 1995.

Parkinson, Frank. *Post-Trauma Stress: Recovery from Hidden Emotional Damage Caused by Violence and Disaster.* Tucson, AZ: Fisher Books, 2000.

Rothbaum, Barbara Olason, Ph.D. *Treating the Trauma of Rape.* New York: Guilford Press, 1997.

Schiraldi, Glenn R. *Post-Traumatic Stress Disorder Sourcebook.* New York: McGraw Hill, 2000.

Sonken, Daniel Jay, and Lenore E. A. Walker. *Wounded Boys, Heroic Men: A Man's Guide to Recovering from Child Abuse.* Avon, MA: Adams Media Corp., 1998.

Terr, Lenore. *Unchained Memories: True Stories of Traumatic Memories, Lost and Found.* New York: Basic Books, 1995.

Vermilyea, Elizabeth G. *Growing Beyond Survival: A Self-Help Toolkit for Managing Traumatic Stress.* Towson, MD: Sidran Press, 2000.

Whitfield, Charles L., M.D. *Memory and Abuse: Remembering and Healing the Wounds of Trauma.* Deerfield Beach, FL: Health Communications, Inc., 1995.

Wright, Leslie Bailey, and Mindy B. Loiselle. *Back on Track: Boys Dealing with Sexual Abuse.* Brandon, VT: Safer Society Press, 1997.

Index

About the Authors

Carolyn Simpson is a therapist at Parkside Psychiatric Services and Hospital in Tulsa, Oklahoma, and has worked in the field of mental health since 1974. Additionally, she teaches psychology and human relations at Tulsa Community College and has written more than twenty books on health-related subjects. She received her bachelor's degree in sociology from Colby College, in Waterville, Maine, and her master's degree in human relations from the University of Oklahoma.

Dwain Simpson is a licensed clinical social worker employed by Hillcrest Medical Center of Tulsa. He also works in private practice in Tulsa, Oklahoma. He received both his bachelor's degree in political science and his master's in social work from the University of Oklahoma. He has practiced social work for more than twenty-four years.

The authors have collaborated on two previous books for the Rosen Publishing Group: *Careers in Social Work* and *Coping with Emotional Disorders.* The couple reside with their three children on the outskirts of Tulsa.